Almost like William Blake, the Sanskrit scholar and writer of repute, Professor Radhavallabh Tripathi has responded to the call of the hour by creating an inter generic "echoing green" text for young adults where a school boy from a drought affected area creates a unique bond with Manavi, a Rajhansini left behind by her own flock. With a delicate sense of humour, the novella goes on exposing ministers, and bigwigs who pay only a lip tribute to noble projects like the one initiated by Salim Ali. The novella is commendable also for its keen insights into the lives of common masses, peasants and other people who have nowhere to go and nothing to spend.

The story is an inter generic mix in the sense that it carries the flavours not only of a fable and an allegory but also of a travelogue and a decent romance. The circus goes to places, even to Moscow where Raghu meets Valentina, and soon after that he succeeds in connecting Manavi to Anant, Manavi's old friend from the flock. We keep dreaming of a universe where men, women and this Cosmos with its great fleet of creatures, great and small, live together in perfect amity. Prof Tripathi has built a Utopia around the notion of the Universe being an interconnected web. Manavi suffers a burn in her own throat when Raghu tells a lie. Such a tender connect has a poetic import of a high order. We have heard stories of saints like Paramahans bearing the marks of lashes on his own back when he saw an English officer thrashing a poor fisherman on the other bank of the river. Tripathi has done justice to many such inter texts which keep flying in the novella with the grace of swans.

—**Anamika**

Recipient of *Sahitya Akademi Award*

Author, poet and critic

MANAVI

A novel for children

Originally written in Sanskrit and translated by

Radhavallabh Tripathi

VANI
PRITHVI

Vani Prakashan Group's imprint
dedicated to the Environment Studies

Paperback First Edition : 2023

VANI PRAKASHAN GROUP
Head Office

4695, 21-A, Daryaganj, New Delhi 110 002, India
Phone : +91 11 23273167 Fax : +91 11 23275710

Registered Bookstores and Offices
Ashok Rajpath, Patna 800 004, Bihar
Coffee House Campus, Mahatma Gandhi Marg, Allahabad 211 001, Uttar Pradesh
Mahatma Gandhi International Hindi University, Wardha 442 001, Maharashtra
36-A, Shakespeare Sarani, Near Rani Birla Girls College, Kolkata-700017, West Bengal

www.vaniprakashan.com
marketing@vaniprakashan.in
sales@vaniprakashan.in

Manavi
Translated by Radhavallabh Tripathi

ISBN : 978-93-5518-826-7
Novel

Illustrated by Anupriya

Price : ₹ 199

Printed at R. Tech Offset Printers, Delhi-110 032

Vani Prakashan's signature motif is created by Artist Maqbool Fida Husain

This Novel is dedicated to Salim Ali.
Salim Ali in the novel is purely imaginary.

Acknowledgements

I have absolutely no words to thank

Anamika, eminent Hindi poet, for having revised my translation of this novel and for taking pains to check the proofs;

Krishna Kumar, eminent educationist, and author, for his very insightful review of the Hindi translation of this novel;

Alok Bhalla and Ashok Upadhyaya : their appreciation came to me as a moral support;

and

Praveen Pandya, promising Sanskrit scholar and thinker, who could understand the inner voices of this novel.

—Radhavallabh Tripathi

1

It is July already and the temperature in Delhi has soared up to forty-five degree Celsius. At Churu in Rajasthan the temperature recorded is fifty degree celsius. Mumbai is searing in summer, Kolkata burning. Temperature in Madras has broken all records. The repercussions of global warming are writ large everywhere...."

Salim Ali was reading this news in the daily News India when his eyes suddenly fell on a heading at the corner of the page –"Swans spotted in a village at Bundelkhand."When he read this news, his eyes widened. Almost holding his breath, he read the news in detail. It read—

"Something beyond our imagination has happened in a small village called Nandanpur in the district of Vidisha near the capital city of Bhopal in Madhya Pradesh. This village lies at the bank of the river Betwa. A rare breed of swans – the Rajhamsa – is spotted here this summer. A flock of more than forty swans of this very rare breed has descended on the bank of the river at the outskirts of this village. Professor Rastogi, a well known ornithologist,who heads the Department of Zoology at the University of Bhopal says that these swans have arrived from Canada.

The village is impoverished and scarcely connected. How these swans could have descended here is a matter of research.

This news unsettled him. He heaved a sigh. His hands were literally trembling as he read the news again.

The sun was rising. Salim Ali could see the orange disc on the horizon from his window.

Suddenly he threw away the newspaper, and telephoned his secretary– 'Panditji! Please come immediately! There is an emergency!'

Bholanath, his Secretary, whom Salim Ali addressed as 'Panditji' lived nearby. He was doing his morning puja when Salim Ali telephoned him. He finished his puja quickly and rushed to the house of his master. His wife Bhamati kept on shouting – 'Wait! Wait!! You have not even taken your breakfast and you have to drop Pankaj to school also!'

Bholanath paid no heed and left the house hurriedly. Bhamati kept on muttering – 'That old man – will you give your life for him! What does he do for you for all your services?'

Bholanath found his sahib seated in a chair, reading the newspaper.

–'Thank God! Nothing has gone wrong!'– He told himself – 'I was afraid he might have been taken ill…'

Salim Ali lived alone in Delhi. Bholanath did everything for him…right from arranging the supply of grocery and other items, to typing his articles and letters and making reservations for his travel.

– 'Panditji, please book my flight to Bhopal immediately!' – Salim Ali said urgently, as he caught sight of Bholanath.

Intrigued at this most unexpected request, Bholanath asked him – 'Has something cropped up suddenly? Is there a lecture in Bhopal? Whom should I contact? Who will make arrangements for your stay?

Salim Ali said – 'Oh Pandit Bholanathji! You really Bholanath incarnate! I am not going to Bhopal!'

Bholanath thought that his sahib had grown old, so his memory was failing. Just moment ago he had said that he was going to Bhopal, and now he says that he is not going to Bhopal!

Salim Ali said – 'I will actually go to Vidisha from Bhopal. There is no airport at Vidisha. My student Rastogi, is there at Bhopal.'

'Yes, yes Sir! Rastogi Sahib is a Professor at Barkatullah University in Bhopal! I have his contact number….'

'Good! Thank God, you are so meticulous. Tell Rastogi to arrange for a taxi at Bhopal… I will proceed to Vidisha directly from Bhopal airport…if Rastogi learns that I am coming, he will himself come to the airport.'

'Shall I accompany you? You are not well…The doctor says you should not be travelling. If at all you have to go, you need to have an assistant.'

'Panditji, you have not taken your breakfast, and you have to drop your son to school. The Panditain must be cursing me for calling you so early. Book me a seat in the plane and go home. I will manage the rest. Don't bother about me—if I see swans, I will become okay. You also have to type my paper on vultures.'

Salim Ali was a great ornithologist. The world respected him for his studies on birds. His counsel was always sought by veterans in the field.

Bholanath went to his cabin and searched for flights. Then he informed Salim Ali –'Sir! there is a flight leaving at ten…a seat is also available—shall I book it?'

'Is there no flight before that?'

'Sahib, it is already seven….'

'OK fine. My return flight should be for this evening. Book a taxi for me for airport just now and please telephone Rastogi.'

Rastogi met him at Bhopal, and he yelled at him – 'Rastogi! Why did you say that the swans have come from Canada? How could you make such a silly statement?'

Put to shame, Rastogi tried to dismiss it with a smile. 'It was a conjecture, Sir!'- he said.

—'You should not make such foolish conjectures. You should read the theory of Anumaana in Indian philosophy! These swans must have come from the Himalayas and in a day or two they might fly back …The rains may arrive any moment. Swans do not stay during rains... and where is the taxi?' he asked impatiently.

—'My car is there, Sir! We can go in that! But before that, take rest, Sir! There is arrangement for your stay at the Government Rest House…'

—'No! No!! It is already the last week of June. Any moment the swans can fly back. If we get late, we may lose the sight!'

It was eleven- thirty in the forenoon. Salim Ali walked swiftly and got in the car even before Rastogi, asking the driver – 'Please start…we will go directly to village Nandanpur in the Vidisha district.'

2

The Betwa flows across Nandanpur. On the banks of the river some forty swans have raised their abode. Out of them some have grown old; some are still young, while some, like Shanku, are just infants.

As July drew close, the crows started making nests. One crow was carrying a blade of grass in his beak. Shanku asked him –'Where are you carrying the straw?'

He said – 'I will raise a nest.'

'Where are our nests?' Shanku went to grandpa and asked him.

Grandpa Suchanchu said – 'We are swans. We do not make nests. The whole world is our nest. The sky is our roof and the earth our bed.'

At this moment, a cloud descended on the top of the mountain.

Anant was the leader of the swans. He was young and very intelligent too. He announced –'With the onset of the monsoon on the first day of Ashadha, the time for our departure is at the door. We must fly back to Mansarovar!'

There was huge hullaballoo in the group. Baby swans were asking – 'Where are we going?'

The breeze blew gently over them, pleased by their cooing. River Betwa laughed through the flow of waves.

'Listen Anant, we have to go all the way to Mansarovar! We need to store some food for the journey. Some geese are expecting. They will deliver their babies soon… how will they fly with us?' – Grandpa Suchanchu wondered.

Anant assured him – 'Everything will be alright. Do not worry. We will fly slowly. We have enough time. The rains will not reach the northern mountains for another month. We will fly at ease and still reach Mansarovar within twenty days. Manavi and I will arrange for everything. Everything will turn out well.'

'Everything will turn out well'— this was the pet sentence Anant would utter to re-assure the members of his group.

Manavi helped him in all types of activities. She was already very busy, trying to soothe the crying babies and assembling the studs of lotuses for food.

Uddanda is good at calculations. He said—'The fifth of this month is an auspicious day. After that there will be plenty of rains for the next ten days….'

Anant called Manavi – 'Manavi! Collect some more studs for the journey… and stop worrying for that boy….'

Raghu is the boy Manavi keeps worrying about. Her companions tell her to forget the boy, 'Manavi, you do not know these humans…they are not reliable…. We are swans. We cannot establish bonds with human beings.'

But Manavi would not part company with Raghu even when the elders of her group reprimanded her.

Constantly she kept worrying for Raghu, "What will happen to him if she goes away from here? She may not be able to meet him again!"

Manavi is very sincere and resourceful. Everyone in the community of swans loved her. But ever since he became friend with Raghu, she has been a laughing stock. Anant tried bringing her to senses several times, 'Manavi! You have started behaving like human beings. It is unbecoming of you. You should break all relations with that lad….' – he would tell her.

'What shall I do, Anant! That boy saved my life… and then, he is so simple…I just can't help liking him!'

Manavi is a little bit lonely in this group of swans. Her mother Varada died just after giving birth to her. Her Papa became an ascetic. Grand pa gave her this name – Manavi. Perhaps because of this she started behaving like manavas –human beings. Often she became pensive. She also worried about the world a lot.

'Why should we poke our beaks in human affairs?'–The other swans would confront her with this question.

Paavani was unwilling to go to Mansarovar. 'Why not stay here itself at Nandanpur?' 'It is peaceful. We are happy here. This river Betwa is beautiful…'

'No, No!'-Tandya interrupted – 'What is here in this village? Dry fields… no crops. Waters are drying up. It will be difficult to trace the stems of lotus in just a few days…'

At this moment Sanchu, the crane, appeared flanking his beak all around. He asked the swans haughtily – 'Where are you people all set to go?'

Suddenly, Saghosha, the frog from the well jumped out and started rattling – 'Tar – Tar---Tar...!Rains are at the door! And you people are going away! There is plenty of water in the well…and tasty insects to eat too…we will stay here eating and drinking all day long. What do you think, Manavi? I have already proposed to you. Marry me and live happily here after.'

Suddenly three boys came running.

Manavi shouted – 'Saghosh! Run, run way. The boys are after you .. They will catch you!'

Saghosh took a deep plunge into the well. The boys cried – 'Oh, he is gone! He has jumped into the well… we have lost a great opportunity.'

Shanku asked Manavi – 'Didi, why are these boys always catching frogs?'

'Frogs provide them their study material. They need frogs.'

'How can frogs teach them? Frogs are fools…How can they be teachers?'

'No Shanku! Frogs are not their teachers. They dissect the frogs to learn about the parts of the body.'

'What kind of education is it? Horrible!'

Manavi was reminded of Raghu. I must go and tell him that we are leaving this place. She told Paavani – 'Paavani, I am going to meet Raghu!'

Paavani was surprised– 'At this hour?'– she said – 'Everybody is getting ready to fly. We are leaving this place.'

'I will not take much time' – Manavi said – 'I will go and comeback.'

'Better ask Anant, he is the leader. He won't allow you to go at this hour.'

Anant said the same thing – 'Going at this hour to see that boy! It is just not proper.'

Manavi's eyes filled with sadness– 'This is the last time, Anant that I will be seeing him, let me go,' – she pleaded.

Anant said – 'OK! If you insist! But don't get late. The group will not wait for you! Even I will not wait for you!'

Manavi thought that he was joking. She flew away.

It was time for departure. All the swans were ready to fly. There were three baby swans -- happily flapping their wings. It is going to be a long journey – they were being told.

'But where is Manavi?'Some of the swans asked.

Grand pa said – 'What to do? Manavi is so much in love with that boy, Raghu…She must have gone to meet him.'

Paavani said – 'Baba, that boy also loves her very much. He even talks to her and understands whatever Manavi says—isn't that wonderful?'

'Everybody is ready? We are about to leave for the Mansarovar!'– Anant made an announcement.

'Come everybody!' Grandpa Suchanchu also called out.

'Here we go! One, two, three…!!' – Tandya cried.

A line of parrots was seen flying over.

'Are these parrots also going to Mansarovar with us?' Shanku asked.

Anant said – 'Oh these poor parrots! How far will they accompany us? They will hardly reach the outskirts of this village and crying tiun tiun they will descend on some tree… Nobody can accompany us till the Manasarovar! We alone can go up to that place…'

Very slowly they were making circles for soaring up above.

'But where is Manavi?' Tandya again asked.

'Manavi will be here any moment. She went with my permission' – Anant said – ' it is alright..'

He was hoping that Manavi come back. He delayed the departure for a while and slowed the speed of the circles he was creating in the sky. As time ticked on, he felt irritated. Manavi was nowhere on the scene.

The young swans were in a hurry. They had already gone ahead. Paavani was becoming restless. She desperately called out–'Manavi, Manavi! Where are you?'

Anant announced again –'Is anybody left? This is the final call!'

But Manavi was still not there. Anant was feeling disappointed. Slowly the group departed.

3

Afternoon had set in when Salim Ali reached Nandanpur with Rastogi. Rastogi had somehow contacted the Patwari[1] of Nandanpur through the District Commissioner of Bhopal. He joined them on the outskirts of the village. On the way the village urchins started running after their car.

They arrived at the bank of river Betwa. The Patwari alighted from the car and looked around.

'The swans are not here!' – He exclaimed in disappointment – 'Only yesterday I spotted the whole flock ....they were around forty. Ever since the news appeared in papers, we are watchful and I take a round here daily. But how could it happen? How can they just disappear?'

Intently looking at the sky, Salim Ali was transfixed. Putting his index finger on his lips he said in a low tone – 'Shsh...keep quiet! The swans will get frightened.'

Rastogi raised his eyes in the direction Salim Ali was looking at. 'Oh, here are they –the swans!' – He cried. Then noticing Salim Ali in a contemplative mood, he shut his mouth and concentrated on the sight in the sky.

---

[1]Head of the village

It was a wonderful sight. Very slowly the swans were scaling the heights in the sky. It seemed as if river Ganga was streaming into the Yamuna.

At this sight Salim Ali took out his hat and saluted the swans thrice, then he started dancing joyfully. Some of the villagers had gathered there by then. Rastogi thought – 'Salim Ali is my guru. He is dancing with his slim body. Shall I dance with my fat body too? I am also very happy at the sight of these swans and feel like dancing. But the village folks are laughing at us. My guru is great; whatever he does is taken in a different light.

The news that Salim Ali was dancing out of joy at the sight of the rare species of swans will appear on Doordarshan and in newspapers tomorrow. 'Professor Rastogi was also dancing with him' - if this also comes in the news, my students at the University will laugh…, and my colleagues will be teasing me.'

By the time Rastogi could decide whether to dance or not, a shining black Ambassador car suddenly appeared on the spot and stopped in front of them. The driver swiftly came out and opened the back door of the car. A gentleman came out. Joining his palms before Salim Ali, he said – 'Good morning Sir! I am Awasthi…Chief Secretary of the State… we did not know that you were coming, we were not properly informed of your arrival. But we are very happy that you have come here. The State of Madhya Pradesh welcomes you Sir! I welcome you on behalf of the honorable Chief Minister of Madhya Pradesh…He has specially ordered me to welcome you. In fact, he himself wanted to meet you, Sir. He is very concerned about the extinction of sparrows in our

State...he would like to seek your guidance in this regard... How to increase the population of sparrows...he is thinking of starting a 'Save the Sparrow Project.'

Salim Ali was still intently looking at the line of swans flying in the sky through his binocular. The line was not visible now. Putting away the binocular, he said – 'Mr. Awasthi, tell your Chief Minister not to worry about the sparrows.... He should better worry about the poor farmers committing suicide and stop deadly pesticides being sprinkled in the fields. If the farmers live, the sparrows live...if the farmers die, the sparrows will also die...'

Saying this he again tried to locate the line of swans which had completely disappeared by now.

Awasthi was taken aback and was looking at Salim Ali with widened eyes. 'Rastogi, let us go' – Salim Ali said— 'I will return by the evening flight...I have seen what was worth seeing, there is no point in staying on.'

Saying this he walked towards the car. Rastogi rushed towards the car and opened the rear door for him. Once Salim Ali settled down in the car, Rastogi asked him – 'Sir, the Chief Secretary is waiting for your response! What should I tell him?'

'Response for what?'

'About your appointment with the Chief Minister, Sir!'

Salim Ali said , 'There is no time, Rastogi. Tell him that I will come some other time. The swans have flown away. I have seen whatever was worth seeing.'

Rastogi heaved a sigh and said ,'Ok, Sir!'

But neither Salim Ali nor anyone else there noticed that one of the members of the group of swans had overstayed at Nandanpur.

4

The swans flew away. Manavi was left alone at Nandanpur.

Manavi had thought that she would just pay a visit to Raghu, see him and come back to join her group which was ready to depart.

She had reached Raghu's house and had called him, cooing in a low tone.

Raghu, a boy of ten yers, had come out. He was looking very sad. But seeing Manavi, he smiled and wondered—'Manavi, you here? This is a very narrow lane, and the boys here are mischievous… they could hurt you, they can throw pebbles.'

Manavi said –'Don't worry, they will not be able to do any mischief… I am in a hurry … we are leaving the place.'

'Where are you going, Manavi?'

'To Manasarovar! Our group is going to depart…I came to say goodbye to you.'

'Oh! You will go away from our village? Why do you have to go?'

'You appear to be sad, Raghu! What is the matter?'

'Manavi! I have not eaten anything for the past two days…There is no food at home…Mother is also fasting…grains are there in bazaar…but we do not have money…I went to the grocery shop to borrow flour. The shopkeeper refused.'

'Why did you not come to me? I would have given you food.'

'You? How could you have given food… you survive just on stalks of lotus. But don't worry,I will do something…I think I will take some job, You know Manavi, the government has a scheme for the victims of famine! But how could you know – these are the affairs of the human world!'

'Come with me,' Manavi told Raghu.

'Come where? Mother is alone in the house… she is running temperature!'

Manavi did not say anything and she started hovering over Raghu.

Suddenly three boys came running and shouted - 'See! the big white bird is flying over Raghu's head! Let us catch it!'

'Come, Raghu!', Manavi said and flew towards the forest. Raghu ran after her.

They came to the forest. River Betwa was flowing in the groves. Her waves made a gurgling sound as they struck the roots of the trees.

Raghu was panting. He shouted,'Manavi! Where are you leading me to? I can't run anymore. We cannot get anything in this forest. It is infested with wild animals!'

Manavi said,'We are very close to the place. Come to this grove.'

On a passage between two hills there stood a mango tree thick with ripened mangoes. Manavi alighted on the tree.

'Oh my God! So many mangoes and all ripe! But I cannot climb the tree! I have no strength left in me!' Raghu said disconsolately.

'I will drop the fruits for you! You pick them up!'

Manavi dropped the fruits from above by hitting on the joints of the ripe mango fruits with her beak. The fruits fell on the ground one by one. Raghu picked up the fruits and started sucking with gusto.

'They are so delicious!' – He exclaimed joyfully- 'I did not know such tasty fruits grew in this jungle!'

'How could you know?' – Manavi said – 'The forest is very dense and dangerous too. Don't ever come here alone.

Because Palash, Karanj and Peepul trees cover this tree – the only mango tree in this area, so it escapes the notice of passers by. I came here in the spring season when this tree was abloom with sprouts… I tasted some sprouts, oh! I did not like the stringent taste…they are not sweet like the lotus stem.'

Raghu said – 'Manavi, taste some mangoes, they are delicious!'

'No, I do not eat mangoes either… lotus stems alone are good for us…Raghu, you take some fruits for your mother.'

Raghu was wearing a pyjama with large pockets, so he stuffed both the pockets with as many mangoes as he could. Manavi laughed at his desperation. Raghu laughed too. Then he started running towards his house. Manavi took flight and shouted from above – 'Raghu! I am going!'

Raghu said – 'What are you saying? Going where?'

'I just told you…we are all going to Mansarovar! In fact, I have overstayed here! I must rush now…otherwise my group will fly away without me!'

Raghu had heard her several times talking about Mansarovar. He said – 'Don't go, Manavi! Mansarovar is far away. The Chinese army is there!'

Manavi laughed. She said – 'What can the Chinese army do to us! We are friends with all the people.'

Raghu was now worried. He said – 'Manavi, I cannot live here without you…Who will get mangoes for me?'

'You will get lots of mangoes, Raghu…Now go home… bye bye!!'

But alas when Manavi reached the dwelling of the swans,

she found it deserted. The swans had left. Two cars were parked nearby. An old man was boarding one of the cars. 'Let us go,' he was saying –'I will return by the evening flight…I have seen what was worth seeing. There is no point staying here.'

There was another man. He said something to the old man sitting in the car. Manavi could not hear what he said. But she heard the old man saying – 'There is no time, Rastogi. …The swans have flown away! I have seen whatever was worth seeing.'

What is this old man saying? The swans have flown away!.

Then Manavi saw that the other man also got into the car and the car started moving. The other car followed it. She recognized the head of the village. He had come to the ground yesterday also. He was walking on the path leading to the village. Some lads of the village had gathered there, they were also going back.

'The swans have flown away. I have seen whatever was worth seeing!' – These words, spoken by the old man were resonating in Manavi's ears. 'How can it be possible?' – She murmured – 'Anant cannot do that – he loves me!'

Manavi hurriedly took a flight over the ground , she scaled the whole ground from above. There was no trace of the swans.

Manavi was horrified. – 'Paavanii, Paavanii!!' she called out loudly.

There was no answer.

'Baba! Baba!' – She called out for her grandpa. And then she shouted in a choked voice– 'Anant! Where are you?'

At this moment, Saghosha, the frog living in the well, jumped out. Seeing Manavi he started rattling – 'Tarr.. Tarrr..! What a pleasure! And what a surprise! All those wicked swans have gone away and you have stayed here for me! I am delighted! I knew that you love me. You can now live with me in the well. It is so cozy inside the well and secure also. It will be such a pleasure…will you marry me now? Really lady, I always thought of marrying in these happy times of rainy season! Marriage in this rains! Turrr… Turrrr…'

Manavi did not say anything, and she alighted on the branch of a banyan tree. It felt like dusk. Had she lost the sense of the time? She went to the jungle with Raghu; but that was not very faraway and she had rushed to this place immediately after dropping a few mangoes for Raghu…No, she did not take so much time…the members of her group should have waited for her a little.

And Anant! – Manavi thought of him. – I had told him that I would come back… 'But don't delay. The group will not wait for you! I would also not wait for you!' Anant had said. I thought he was joking. On other occasions Anant had waited for her.

How will she stay here alone? Manavi was worried. It was dark now. Sometimes a wicked owl would visit this place. With his eyes shining in the dark, he would search for small birds to kill and devour them. Once he was about to attack and take away Shanku. Anant and Tandya fought with him and drove him away. And what about the vultures? They are deadlier. What if they come and attack her? She will die here…the swans of her group will forget her….

Manavi was scared. She concealed herself in a trove in the tree. She was hungry but she did not feel like eating anything.

I have ruined my life for a boy – Manavi thought. She could not sleep the whole night. It was hot inside the trove. She dozed off for some time in the last quarter of the night.

'Oh, so Manavi is really gone!' - She heard a familiar voice.

Suddenly Manavi was awake. Was she dreaming and hearing the voice of Raghu? Hurriedly she came out and glanced below.

Raghu was really there! He was going back slowly. 'Raghu!' Manavi called out. Raghu turned back and saw her on the tree.

'Oh Manavi, you! I thought you have left! I could not thank you for those exquisite mangoes yesterday. Mother loved them! I wanted to thank you, so I came here before going to school. Then I remembered that you were to leave our village. You did not go then! I am delighted to see you here!'

'You are delighted, but what about me, Raghu!…'

'What about you, Manavi?'

Manavi did not reply.

'Manavi, have the members of your group left?'

'Yes, they have left!'

'Oh, so they did not take you with them?'

'No Raghu, I got late yesterday…It was time for departure …they must have been waiting for me but by the time I came here, they had left…every one of them.'—she said sadly.

Raghu was aghast. He understood now that something wrong had happened. Manavi lost her group because of him.

'Manavi, you could have flown with speed to join them...'

'I do not know the way, Raghu. Only Anant and grandpa know the way to Mansarovar. I searched for them all around. I called them. But I think it was too late...'

'Manavi, I can tell you the way to Mansarovar...you can still go! All the ways are described in our geography book and maps are also given...look! You fly towards north from here...Bhopal is this side and this side is Vidisha—you go that way to Mandsaur...and from there to Haridwar...'

Manavi viewed Raghu curiously. 'Raghu, you know so many things but how would I know which city I have reached? I cannot read nor can I talk to human beings. Seeing me alone any man will catch me or kill me. All men are not as simple as you are. You have a pure heart like us swans.'

Raghu was worried. 'What will you do here then?' – he said, 'Come and live with us. I will take care of you!'

Manavi said – 'I will stay here. There are wicked boys in your neighborhood.'

Raghu felt very sorry for Manavi. 'What should I do for you then?' - he murmured out of pity.

'Raghu, don't worry' – Manavi said – 'You come here daily in the evening. I will somehow pass the days. I feel re-assured in your company.'

Raghu sat on a slab of stone. Manavi came down and sat on his lap. Raghu stroked her back tenderly. Manavi dozed off in his lap.

5

The month of July was over. It was August now. All these days it had not rained. The heat of the summer was unbearable. The residents of Nandananpur glanced over the sky to see if the rain clouds had arrived. There was no sign of clouds.

On the banks of Betwa, lotus flowers were still blooming. Manavi roamed around there and suspecting some danger she immediately alighted on the Bargad tree. She remained depressed. The memories of Anant, Paavani, Shanku and grandpa come to her again and again. But she tried to remain calm and looked forward to Raghu's regular visits. Raghu did come every day. He expected Manavi to play with him like before. Manavi remained passive.

And then the bond of friendship between Raghu and Manavi was rekindled all of a sudden. Once Manavi got hurt when a boy threw a stone on her. Raghu saw her lying on the ground. He lifted her in both his hands and asked – 'Are you alright?'

'Yes' – Manavi said – 'Now it is ok.'

Raghu was surprised. 'What a wonder!' – he said – 'You speak our language!' – he said.

'No!' - Manavi said – 'I do not speak your language. You understand what I say.'

'My name is Raghu. What is your name?'

'My name is Manavi!' she said laughingly.

'Beautiful name. And you speak so sweetly.'

'I speak only for you, and not for other human beings. You saved my life. We are friends now.'

From that day onwards their friendship prospered. Raghu loved to talk to Manavi while Manavi rejoiced in chatting with him. Nobody could hear what they were talking. Some boys spotted Raghu conversing with Manavi and they thought that Raghu had gone mad.

'If I had not overstayed that day – I would have been at Mansarovar today,' Manavi was thinking.

The crows were making nests on the banyan tree where she lived. She was terribly upset by their harsh tweets. There were some wicked crows amidst them, always laughing at her or mocking her: 'Look at the white lady' – someone amongst them would say – 'She has been deserted by her group. These swans – they are so proud and they are always seen fighting against each other. They are not as social as we crows are!'

Manavi was afraid of them. She thought they would surely attack her some day with their hard beaks. Memories of her family came back to her at such moments. They must be rejoicing now at Manasarovar. Babhru had two chicks. How lovely they were! It is already one month since I have been left alone here… they must have grown up now. They were as small as the crows then… now they must have become small ducks…Remembering grand pa, her eyes were filled with tears. 'I may not live after this winter' —he used to say—'it is better that I give up this body at Mansarovar!'

Then she remembered Anant. He would often tell her– 'Leave the company of that human boy, Manavi!' I did not listen to him and now I have landed in this trouble!

'Have the members of my group forgotten me by now? No, that was not possible… we swans do not have weak memories like humans…Anant really loves me, he cares for me.. He must have been very upset when I did not come on time. I had said that I would come back in a few minutes,but I got late. He must have waited, and might have said— 'Manavi will be coming back soon. She went with my permission… everything will be fine.'

But then, he had also threatened her that if she delayed, the group would fly away. And he had left. Her group flew away. Nothing could be done now.

That was my mistake --- I got late …Tandya and Paavani, they might have got married…and Shanku.. is he still as innocent? Seeing the clouds she would think that they are elephants.

Remembering Shanku, Manavi started laughing

'Manavi, What happened !'

Manavi was startled. Oh, Raghu was calling. She descended on a lower branch of the tree and asked – 'When did you come, Raghu?'

'I have been calling you for a long time but you were not listening! I looked up to you for so long that my neck is aching. You were weeping and then laughing. What happened, Manavi?'

'Nothing Raghu, I was remembering my family.'

'What can I do for you, Manavi?'– Raghu was thinking– 'Because of me, she got separated from her family.'

'What should I do for you, Manavi? All this has happened because of me!'

'What can you do, Raghu? One month is already gone by. Remaining three months will also pass like that. After that, the members of my group will come back to this village. You better look after yourself. I do not see happy conditions here at your village too.'

'You are right, Manavi! The month of Shravan has arrived and there are no rains. There will be no crop if it goes on like this. All hopes for us are gone. Many people have left for Bhopal. I told mother – 'Let us go to Vidisha, Rammu Mama is there. We will take Manavi with us. But mother said she would not leave the village.'

Manavi sighed and said–'I too will not leave the village –After Shravan, it is Bhadrapada and then Aashvin and then Kaartik.. after that may be in Aagrahayan or Maagha, the members of my group will come back. I will wait for them.'

6

The month of August was almost over.

Will the members of my group return in September or in October? Manavi used to wonder. May be this year they will search for another dwelling. What will happen to me if they do not come? Absorbed in her worries, she was counting days.

Oneday, Raghu came to Manavi's grove and told her—'Manavi, it is Janmashtami today. There will be a keertan in the temple. I am the main singer in the keertan mandali. It is holiday at our school. Keertan will start at 3 in the afternoon. Do come and listen to the keertan. You will feel better.'

'No Raghu, tolling of the bells in the temple makes my heart thump…It is such a sharp sound. Moreover, I do not know when it will be three in the afternoon, and also I am afraid of the village boys, they always try to catch me or throw stones at me.'

'Don't be afraid! There is a big Peepal tree in front of the temple. You can remain hidden there. When the shadow of this banyan tree touches the edge of the bank of the river, it will be three in the afternoon…I am going….my harmonium is lying at Deepesh's house...I have to practice for the keertan also... come to the temple at three o'clock sharp!'

Saying this, he ran away.

Manavi remained seated on the banyan tree. The sun rose high in the sky. She was thinking – 'Because of Raghu, I am separated from my group. Had I made it that day, I would have been in the Mansarovar spending happy times with the members of my group...What to do now? Shall I go to the temple as Raghu says?'

In her reverie, she was overcome by slumber and she had a dream – she was in Mansarovar and all the swans were floating in the water. She was sitting all alone on the bank, imploring to the swans – 'Let me come here, let me join you...!'

Uddanda, raising his beak, roared – 'Hey! How can you join our group now? You belong to that boy ...you are Manavi only, go back to Nandanpur! There is no place for you here!'

Tandya also rebuffed – 'Go back, Manavi, go back! You were not happy with us! Now you must be happy there in Nandanpur. What is there in that village...now you might not even be getting lotus stems to eat...the farmers are committing suicide there ...the waters are drying up...you see all this and remain happy?'

Dalbhya says – 'And the shrill shrieks of the ducks – so unmusical – you listen to them! And the rattling of the crows...that Kalu – the wicked crow, will kill you someday.'

They started laughing at her. Dalbhya said out of pity —'What have you done, Manavi? What did you get in the company of those human beings?'

But Paavani re-assured Manavi. She said – 'Manavi, don't worry..you come… join us back…'

Manavi said – 'I will come…I will join you people again… Where is Anant? He will allow me….'

Uddanda yelled – 'Anant is no more the leader! He is dead. I am the leader now and I don't allow you to join back!'

'You are a liar! It is not possible.' – Manavi says.

'You have called me a liar! Take this then!' – saying this Uddanda suddenly jumped on the bank of the lake and started attacking Manavi with his beak. Shanku cried – 'Sir! Sir!! don't kill Manavi, please don't…'

Paavani cried – 'Manavi! fly away, fly away. This Uddanda is very cruel. He has killed Anant, he will kill you too!'

Manavi implored – 'Please don't kill me, don't, don't! But he attacked her with his beak. His beak felt like an iron rod, falling heavily on Manavi's body, and the sound of 'Tan... tan...tanaatan' was being produced on each fall.

Tan…tan..tanaatan --- this sound aroused Manavi from slumber.

'Oh, I was dreaming!'– she said to herself – 'I slept throughout the day! What an absurd dream! We swans never quarrel like this! Seems my mind is getting corrupted due to this deep association with human beings…How can Uddanda become so cruel? And how could each attack on my body produce a sound of tan—tan?'

Tan, Tan , Tan…....tanaatan..

Oh, the same sound again! The sound is actually coming from somewhere. It is afternoon already. The shadow of the banyan tree is touching the edge of the bank of the river. Oh! so, it is the sound of tolling bells in the temple. Raghu had asked me to come to the temple when the shadow of the tree touches the edge of the bank. What should I do? Shall I go to the temple? If I stay here, I may be seeing another horrible dream.

Manavi stayed transfixed for a while.

Gopal Govind Hare Murare

He Deenbandho...

Oh, Raghu is singing...What a melodious voice! I must go to the temple then! I am not feeling well. There is no swan here to give me company. There is nobody who cares for me here except Raghu. If I avoid him also, I am lost. May be I will feel better after listening to the keertan in the temple.

Thinking this, Manavi got ready to go. – 'Here I go' – she said and flew towards the west. Within three minutes she was in front of the village temple. She alighted on a branch of the Peepal tree facing the temple.

The keertan had just begun in the temple. Raghu had a very soft voice flowing like a fountain. When he took the alap in high pitch, it seemed as if a cuckoo is cooing ...Manavi was elated. 'Raghu was right' —she said to herself, 'around the temple I feel better.'

Raghu song on a perfect note. But when the accompanists repeated his lines, two or three amongst them went out of tune. Some girl there were almost shrieking and not singing.

Listening to the keertan, Manavi was amused.

It was evening now. Darkness was descending on the top of the temple and on the top of the trees now. The soft and warm rays of the sun were touching Manavi. The sun was winding up his rays and descending down the horizon. It looked like a red ball fallen on the ground. Then darkness started covering that red ball. The ball dimmed. Manavi saw the ball sinking below the earth, it was visible three -fourth first, then half and then only the top of it could be seen. Then it disappeared.

'I must go now' – Manavi thought – 'but will it be proper to go without seeing Raghu, He invited me … He must know that I was here and listened to his keertans.'

The sound of keertan had stopped. The group of boys and girls singing keertan were now coming out.

Manavi saw Raghu amongst them and she was delighted. She could recognize the boys and girls of his group, she also knew their names…The boys coming with Raghu were Devesh and Shravan and the girls following them are Sheela and Vimla…

Manavi called Raghu – 'Raghu! Raghu!!'

Passing below the peeple tree, Raghu was startled. Oh, this is Manavi calling me! He looked upward.

'Manavi! You are here? When did you come?'

'I came when you started the keertan…'

The boys and girls were surprised. – 'Raghu! What a wonder! This bird --- this swan …he is talking to you…!'

'She is a female swan – don't say he' – Raghu admonished.

'How do you know?' – Sheela asked.

'I will call her by her name and she will answer. Then you will understand that she is a female, OK?' – saying this, Raghu called Manavi – 'Manavi, are you hearing me?'

'Yes Raghu, I can hear you,' – Manavi said.

The boys were astonished. 'This swan! He is really talking to Raghu!' – they said.

Raghu told them furiously – 'Haven't I told you she is a female! She is Manavi – a lady...don't humiliate her!'

'Oho ho! As if she is your wife or beloved!' – Sheela joked.

'Raghu, ask her to call me by my name!' – Devesh said.

Manavi! This is Devesh! Call him by his name!'

Devesh! How are you, Devesh?' – Manavi said aloud.

The whole group was amused and amazed. Sheela also said 'Raghu! Ask her to call me also!'

Raghu said – 'Manavi! This is Sheela, she is also my fast friend! Call her!'

Manavi called – 'Sheela, Sheela!!'

The boys and girls were laughing. Manavi too was amused. Devesh said – 'We are getting late. My mother will be angry... let us go home.'

Raghu was worried for Manavi. He asked her – 'Manavi, how will you go to your place? It is dark now!'

Manavi said – 'No problem. I can fly back up to my place.'

'It is dark Manavi! – That owl – he may spot you – you come with us...these are all my friends, they will not harm you ...and how long will you stay there alone? Mother says that there are ghosts on the banyan tree...and the nests of those crooked crows...it is not good for you...Come to my house.'

The boys and girls also said – 'Manavi, come with us! We will take care of you, nobody can harm you then.'

Manavi was in a fix. 'Should I do that? I am a swan, I should not live with human beings…' she thought.

Raghu implored again—'What are you thinking, Manavi? You stay with us till your group returns to Nandanpur.'

Manavi thought for a while and then said reluctantly—'OK, Raghu, I'll go'.

The boys and girls were clapping their hands with joy. They were telling each other curiously – 'Did you hear? She said – I will go … she is an intelligent bird…'

Manavi started hovering over Raghu. Boys and girls rushed behind her. Thus, they reached Raghu's house.

7

Time runs at a slow pace at Nandanpur. The farmers could not sow seeds this year because there were no rains. With eyes wide open, everybody looks up to the sky for clouds. Sometimes a stray cloud does appear and then it scatters away like the hope of the farmers. The farmers had taken loan for cultivating the lands and had purchased the seeds and fertilizers, but all in vain. Now there will be no crop, how will they survive with their families... and how will they repay their loan?—All of them were ridden with worries.

Manavi was waiting for her group to return. The rainy season passed by without a trace of rain. Then came autumn. Manavi still visited the banks of Betwa river for her food of lotus stems. She returned to spend the night at Raghu's house. She did enjoy the company of Raghu and his friends now and eagerly went daily to her old dwelling to find out if there is any trace of her group coming back.

In the evening when the boys came to play with Raghu, Manavi mostly sat on the Neem tree outside Raghu's house. When Raghu insisted, she alighted on the ground, the boys tried to touch her and to hold her in their hands. Raghu was very cautious. He would ask them to stay away.

Autumn passed by. The festival of Deepawali was nearing. There were no crops. Then famine was declared. The village people did not light lamps on Deepawali. The young and adults went to Bhopal to stage dharna and agitation. Nandanpur looked deserted.

The news of drought prevailing in the whole area surrounding Vidisha and many areas of Bhopal slowly reached Delhi. A correspondent of the newspaper called *The India News* visited Nandanpur for coverage.

His name was Suryamohan. He roamed around the village and was depressed to see the situation. People appeared to be sad. But seeing something strange happening in a lane, he stood spell- bound.

There were four boys and two girls forming a circle, at the centre of which on a wooden stool sat a swan. The boys were caressing the swan. When they tried to touch her, one of the boys tried to prevent them from doing so. The boys told that boy—'Raghu, ask her to call you by name…'

That boy asked the swan—'Manavi, call me!'

The swan started calling in a melodious voice – 'Raghu, Raghu!'

The boys clapped. Suryamohan was amused. He mixed himself in that circle. When the boys and girls clapped, he also started clapping. Then he addressed the boys—'Hello, where did you get her …I mean this talking swan?'

Raghu protested and said, 'She is not a swan. She is Manavi—a lady.'

'What is your name?'

'My name is Raghu.'

'OK Raghu, so you talk to Manavi and she answers?'

'Yes...where are you from?'

'I am Suryamohan, I am a correspondent in a newspaper —India News. So, where did you learn the language of birds?'

'From nowhere, Manavi talks to me and I understand her.'

'Raghu! Tell him that I learnt the language of birds from my teacher Sharda Prasad, who is an ornithologist!' 'Sheela whispered in Raghu's ear.

Sharda Prasad is Sheela's father. He teaches Zoology in ourschool. He is very influential. He knows many leaders. Raghu cannot go against Sheela, so he told Suryamohan— 'I learnt the language of birds from my teacher Sharda Prasad, who is an ornithologist!'

Suryamohan laughed and said – 'That is great! You are very intelligent, Raghu! You will become a leader one day! I will publish you photograph in my newspaper.'

Then he took out his camera and said – 'OK Raghu, now you hold Manavi in your hands...as if she is your beloved... you kiss her on her beak.'

Raghu did what he said. The girls and boys surrounded Raghu and stood smiling for the photo.

'Raghu, you are not smiling. Smile please and give a tender touch to Manavi!'—Suryamohan said.

Raghu smiled. There was a sound of click-click from the camera. Then Suryamohan said – 'Thank you!'

Suddenly, Manavi's beak staggered on Raghu's cheek and she fell down. Raghu saw that she was breathing heavily, the pupils of her eyes had turned upwards.

Raghu panicked. – 'Manavi, what happened, Manavi?' he asked her anxiously – 'Are you unwell?'

With great pain, Manavi told him – 'Raghu, take me out of here, take me to the river bank.'

Raghu shouted at the gathering – 'Move away, move away! Manavi is not well, how many times have I told you to remain at a distance from her, she suffocates because of your breathing.'

Then he told Suryamohan – 'You also please go away! All this has happened because of you .'

Holding Manavi in his hands, Raghu then ran towards the river.

Reaching her old abode, Manavi was revived. She said in a low voice – 'Raghu, leave me here!'

Raghu was worried. He asked – 'What happened, Manavi? You were laughing… Everyone was happy. Suddenly you became ill.'

Manavi said – 'You lied Raghu! Why did you say that you learnt the language of the birds from Sharada Prasad?'

Raghu said – 'What could I do? Sheela told me to say so.'

'But that was a lie!'

'That's true, Manavi! I committed a sin.'

'Because of your speaking a lie I was burnt. Look at my throat. Your lie burnt my throat.'

Raghu saw that there was a mark of burn on her long beautiful neck.

He stood aghast.

'Manavi, really I did not know that my lie will hurt you so much…I will never tell a lie in future.'

8

"Deepavali has arrived. Darkness, however, prevails in the villages of Bundelkhand. River Betwa has dried up. It has not rained this year too. There is drought everywhere. The farmers could not sow so no crop this year. Families of the farmers are starving. The Government has not done anything for compensation."

Salim Ali was reading this news item in the newspaper *India News*. Suddenly his eyes rested on a news at the right hand corner of the page. Looking at the heading, he started reading the news with curiosity. The heading was –"A Female Swan Becomes the Beloved of a Village Boy". The news read like this –

"Eighty kilometers away from Bhopal, in the village Nandanpur of Vidisha district, a miracle has happened. ***India News*** *had given extensive coverage of the famine and starvation widespread in this area. Amidst all the gloom, something like a fairy tale has occurred in Nandanpur. A female swan has become the beloved of a ten-year-old boy. She talks to this boy – Raghu. They are intimate with each other; they speak to each other. The female swan has even started speaking like human beings. Our correspondent Suryamohan has visited the spot and witnessed everything. Raghu says that the swan is a*

lady and she is his beloved from the past lives....In fact, she is so attached to Raghu that she quit the company of her group which has left for Mansarovar three months back...Raghu, the boy who looks after the she-swan says that he learnt the language of the birds from the well-known ornithologist in the area Shri Sharada Prasad, who teaches Zoology in a school at Nandanpur."

Reading the news, Salim Ali started laughing and said to himself – "These newspaper-wallas! They write anything! I saw with my own eyes that all the swans from the village flew away – not a single one stayed back. And suddenly a correspondent goes there and sees a swan talking in human language! Ha..ha..ha!!"

At this moment, Bholanath came to his room from the adjacent cabin. He saw that his boss was laughing aloud with a newspaper in his hand. 'Because of old age, Sahib has gone out of his mind and he laughs any time without rhyme or reason'- he thought – 'But if Sahib is laughing, I should laugh too!'. So, he also started laughing. Seeing him laugh, Salim Ali stopped laughing and asked him in a stern voice – 'Pandit ji, why are you laughing?'

Bholanath said – 'Sahib, I saw you laughing, so I started laughing. There is no other reason behind my laughter.'

Salim Ali said – 'You are my secretary. Does that mean that you should do whatever I do?'

'No Sahib! You are a great person. How can I do what you do?'

'OK...I am laughing at the foolishness of these news-paper-walllas... see what a fairy tale they have woven! All rubbish! - A female swan becomes the beloved of the village boy! Read it yourself and enjoy!'

Saying this, Salim Ali handed over the newspaper to Bholanath.

Bholanath took the newspaper and read the news in his cabin. Reading the news about the boy Raghu and Manavi--the she-swan, he remembered his younger brother Kalanath.

Even as small boy, Kalanath displayed his skills and interest in acrobatics. He was least interested in studies, but he played several games and excelled in sports. He had already joined a circus company by the time Bholanath became the private secretary of Salim Ali. He learned a lot of tricks at the circus company. The owner of the company was extremely pleased with his performance. Now Kalanath was the manager of Nataraj Circus Company.

For the past three years, contact between Bholanath and Kalanath had remained snipped. Vandana was the reason behind this. She was the only daughter of Ramnath Bajaj—an industrialist. She went to see a show of Natraj Circus Company where Kalanath was working, heard him make announcements and also saw him perform some feats. This made her fall in love with him. On a day when there was no circus show, Kalanath accepted her invitation to visit her house – a big mansion in Kailaspuram –a posh colony in Delhi. There Vandana conveyed her love to Kalanath. They started meeting. Vandana would also go to meet Kalanath when he would be giving shows in other towns. Then Ramanath Bajaj, her father, invited Kalanath to his house and told him plainly – 'If you wish to marry my daughter, you will also have to live in my house as a *gharjamai*, you will have to leave the circus company and look after my business.'

Kalanath told him plainly – 'I will not leave the circus and will not live with you as gharjamai.' Vandana was very sad at this. She kept on weeping for many days. Then her father called Bholanath and told him - 'You please try to bring your younger brother to his senses'. He also gave lucrative offers to Bholanath. 'I have branches of my company all over the country. I will make you the general manager of any branch you wish to join' – he said. Then Bholanath talked to Kalanath. But Kalanath was firm on his decision. Bholanath got angry with him, and said- 'Do whatever you wish. From this day onwards, I am no longer your elder brother and you no longer my younger brother.' Bholanath's wife, Bhamati tried her best to reconcile the two brothers. She remonstrated Bholanath on breaking relations with his brother. However, the bond of fraternity between the two brothers had remained suspended all these years and had revived only recently.

Natraj Circus had come to Delhi this year. Kalanath himself telephoned Bholanath. He asked Bholanath if he could come to pay respect to his Bhabhiji.

'OK', Bholanath said. Kalanath came in the evening. Bholanath was in his office. Kalanath talked to his Bhabhi and his nephew. He was telling them stories about various cities in India that he had seen. When Bholanath returned home, Kalanath touched his feat. Seeing him, Bholanath's anger melted away and he embraced his younger brother. The dialogue between them re-started. They talked about their school days and childhood.

Bholanath's wife was listening to Kalanath's stories with rapt attention. He had visited many countries outside India, so many cities in India he had seen! – 'Look! What a knowledgeable person Kala Babu is!' – She told Bholanath – 'He knows about the whole world! What do you know about the world? You know only about the files of that Ali Salim..'

'I know so many things about birds because of my association with Sahib'- Bholanath said with pride—'Kala might not be knowing the difference between a duck and a swan! I know!'

'So what?' – Bhamati said – 'What is the use of knowing about birds? You do not know what the good shopping places even in Delhi are. Kalababu knows about markets in all big cities!'

Seeing his brother thus chided by his sister-in-law, Kalanath was amused. He started laughing, and then defending his brother he said - 'Salim Ali is a great man! He is respected all over the world!'

Bholanath boastfully said – 'Kala, you do not know one thing. My Sahib is a great scholar, but even he learns things from me!'

'Acchcha? What things have you taught him?' – Bhamati interrupted him.

'I learnt Sanskrit up to Shastri level in Gurukul. Therefore Sahib calls me Panditji. Once he asked me – Panditji, I want to learn from you… give me a write-up about the swans in Sanskrit Shastras. I wrote an article on swans in Sanskrit literature and gave it to him. You know, Kalanath, he read that article and was very impressed. He said -- 'Panditji! you are a learned man! This article should be published in a good journal with your name as the author!'

'Right, right!' – Kalanath said. Then he told his sister-in-law – '*Bhabhi*! Dada had leant many texts by heart when we were in Gurukul -- Gita, Amarkosha and what not!'

Bholanath was further encouraged. He started telling about various categories of swans – Kadamba, Kalahamsa, Rajahamsa etc. along with their features.

Till now, Bholanath was cross with his younger brother. Now both the brothers felt the old affinity and affection.

'Dada! From tomorrow starts our circus at Delhi. These are the VIP passes of the premier show. Please come with Bhabhi and Pankaj. I will get you seats in the front row.' Saying this, Kalanath handed over three passes to Bholanath.

Bholanath did not have any interest in circus, neither did Bhamati had. But she had more regard for Kalanath than her husband. She said – 'We will definitely come to see your circus! I am sure, Pankaj will enjoy it!'

Pankaj was the five-year old son of Bholanath and Bhamati.

So, Bholanath went to see the circus run by his brother the very next day with his wife and Pankaj. Seeing the wonderful tricks and acrobatics, Bhamati was amazed. Pankaj was thrilled and was laughing all the time. He liked the joker especially. Seeing the monkeys riding the lions, he started to clap. The dance of the bears he found specially delightful. When a lady was riding a motorcycle inside the well of death, he was awe-struck and grabbed his mother. Bhamati embraced her son. She was very pleased to see him enjoying the show.

When the show was over, Kalanath himself came to meet them. He touched the feet of Bholanath and his sister-in-law.

Bhamati was all praise for him. She said – 'Bhaiya, what *kamaal* you do! You should ask your brother to join your circus and do stuff here... it will be better than his sitting all the time in the office of Mr. Mali Mas....

'Arre, Arre! Why you are you distorting the name of my sahib...he is Salim Ali!' – Bholanath interjected.

'OK, Salim Ali, what did you get serving him all these years? See your younger brother! How many people work under him... he is the boss here. So many young men and young ladies – he is their boss and he owns lions and elephants ...You are simply Bholanath and he is Kalanath! That is the difference...He knows so many skills while you don't have any!'

Bholanath always enjoyed the tantrums of his wife. She complained and made all sorts of allegations when she was happy with him. She spoke many bitter and odd things but she was a good woman at heart.

Bhamati was chattering again – 'So many years have gone by but this husband of mine did not take me even to a cinema...Now we have seen circus at least... that too due to the grace of his brother!' – Then she told Kalanath – 'Bhaiya, you should marry now... a good wife will help you in managing this the circus better.'

Kalanath laughed loudly.

'Where is Kalanath now?' Bholanath was thinking. 'I will go to Maharashtra from Delhi'-- he had said. He also had named the city in which the circus would run the shows. Bholanath had forgotten the name of the city.

No…it was not Mumbai… it was some small city he had named…I am sure it will be difficult to contact him.'

Sitting in his cabin, Bholanath dialed Kalanath's cell phone number. It was forenoon. Kalanath was normally free at this hour. From afternoon onwards he would become very busy. The first show starts in the afternoon.

Kalanath had given him his cell phone number. 'In whatever city I am, you can contact me on this number '– Kalanath had told him. It has now been three months since he left Delhi. Bholanath could not contact him all these months. But he was happy that the relations between him and Kalanath had revived. He tried to contact Kalanath, but his cell phone always remained switched off.

But this time the bell went on ringing and Bholanath could hear the voice of his brother from the other end– 'Hello!'

'Kala! I am Bholanath speaking.'

'Oh, Dada! *Pranam*! *Pranam*!!' – Kalanath said with glee.

'Is everything OK?'

'Nothing is OK Dada… you are happy doing a good job with such a great men as Salim Ali Sahib…Running a circus is hazardous!'

'Why? What happened? At Delhi you were doing good business! '

'Yah, Delhi was better. I told you that we were scheduled to give shows in Maharashtra… we came to Mumbai from Pune and the journey was horrible--- one of our lions became ill. He is the main attraction of our circus. He carried a couple of monkeys with their babies on his back in the show…

Now something went wrong with him, seeing the monkeys he starts roaring frightfully; the monkeys are afraid of him now. The trainer is unable to understand his change in behavior.'

'Where are you in Maharashtra now?'

'We are at Ullasnagar…It is a good city, but people do not come to see circus. I am unable to meet the expenses here… This television, it has become disastrous for us… To add salt to the injury, these save-the-animals business people are always after us now! We have two lions, three elephants and one bear. We care for them like our own family members. But ever since the save-the-animals committee gave a memorandum to the government; the government issued an order for all the circus companies, disallowing them to keep wild animal. We can keep only parrots and other birds. But what should I do with parrots? They are good for nothing ...people come to see the lions….'

'Right, right!'

'Even the parrots became a problem. I have three parrots. Now they are quite old. They can only speak 'Ram, Ram'. Once some minister from the previous government came to see our show. After seeing the show, he gave a speech on the spot itself. He praised our circus, but then said – 'Everything else is Ok, but the parrots in your circus company say – Ram Ram! This is not proper. This is violation of secularism!' So I told the trainer of the parrots to train the parrots to say 'Ram and Rahim'. But the parrots would not say 'Rahim'. Tell me Dada, what can I do to make the parrot say Rahim? The trainer says that one of the parrots was taught to sing a film song– '*Yaallaa Yallaa dil le gayi*', so he can try make him speak *Yaa Allaah by splitting yallaa….*'

'Listen, Kala! Did you read *India News* of today?'

'No, Dada! Where do I get time to read newspapers?'

'Listen, I want to tell you something. There is a news item for you.'

Then Bholanath read out the news from the newspaper about the female swan who had become the beloved of a village boy. After that he said – 'The parrots and *mainas*, whatever they say, will not be of interest to people. We have them in our homes and we all make them speak. But if a swan – a *Rajhansa* – speaks in the language of human beings, it will be taken as a miracle. You go to that village and somehow purchase that swan! People in that village are very poor. The village is famine struck. So, they will surely sell the swan!'

Kalanath said – 'It is not easy to keep birds. They often become ill. They get infected easily, and bird doctors are not easily available. Then who will train the swan? We do not have a trainer for swans…But one thing is good, the save-the-animals committee people will not object to our keeping a swan. Their objection is about our keeping lions and elephants… I will note down the name of the village and see if I can go there…Everything else is alright? How are Bhabhi and my dear Pankaj? My pranams to Bhabhi and my blessings to Pankaj…Pranam, Dada…'

9

Suhagini Devi is Raghu's mother. She is an unfortunate lady. Her husband died in an accident when Raghu was about to be born. He was crushed by a truck. People say that it was not an accident; it was a conspiracy against him. He owned a good plot of land for cultivation, close to Betwa River. It yielded plenty of crops. After his death, Ghumman, Suhagini's *devar* (the younger brother of her husband), captured the land forcibly. Suhagini Devi was impoverished. She had one cow. The cow was named Gangi. This year Gangi gave birth to a calf. Raghu loves this calf. He also recognizes Raghu and calls him by bellowing 'ambo, ambo!!' Raghu has named this calf Golu. Golu remains tied with a rope all night. Early in the morning Suhagini Devi unties the knot from his neck and Golu rushes to his mother Gangi. Milk oozes out from the udders of Gangi and Golu nabs his mouth quickly to suck them. After some time, Golu is removed from his mother and tied with a rope again and then Suhagini Devi milks the cow. She forcefully makes Raghu drink most of the milk Gangi yields daily. She makes tea for herself with very little milk. Since Manavi has arrived in their house, Raghu rushes to give her his share of milk and drinks the leftover from the same glass.

Suhagini Devi is very upset about this. She hates Manavi. She somehow supported herself and her son by working as a maid in two or three houses. There was nobody at her parent's house except one younger brother, Ramsevak, who lived in Vidisha. He also lived in very straightened condition and come to Nandanpur only once on the day of *Rakhi*. This year he did not come even on *Rakhi* and there was no news from him. 'Has he also forgotten me?' This thought made Suhagini Devi very upset. To add salt to the injury, her son brought this swan in the house which was a sheer burden on her. She kept on cursing Manavi. 'Arre, will you give your life for this bloody bird?'—Raghu laughed. 'I have already given my life and soul to her.'

It was not easy to get even dry grass and fodder for Gangi now-a-days. Suhagini Devi worked as a maid at the house of Ishvari Prasad, who used to give her fodder free for Gangi. But as the crops failed this year, he did not have fodder to feed even his own cows.

Raghu rose early in the morning these days and took Gangi to the outskirts of the village. There in the meadows under the shades of groves some grass way still left. Gangi would roam around there to graze. Three or four other cows also came to graze. Before dusk, Gangi got restless for Golu, and she would return to the house mooing loudly and rush to her shade. She would start licking Golu and he would put his mouth to her udders.

That day Gangi did not return. Dark shadows were descending over the village. Suhagini Devi called her son and said – 'Raghu, go and look for Gangi, she should have been here long ago but there is no trace of her!'

Raghu looked around everywhere for Gangi. Groping for his way in the dark, he also reached the outskirts. There was a dreadful silence everywhere. Some light from twinkling stars and that's all. Gangi was not to be seen anywhere. Raghu called aloud– 'Gangi! Gangi!'

The village was surrounded by the Vindhyachal mountains. Raghu's call echoed all around – 'Gangi! Gangi!!' As if the hills were also calling Gangi.

It was very unusual. Gangi always responded to his call by bellowing hambaa, hambaa! Gangi was surely not here – otherwise she would call me back – Raghu thought.

Utterly exhausted, he returned home. 'Mother, Gangi is nowhere to be seen! What will happen now, Golu seems very hungry; he does not take anything except Gangi's milk and Manavi… what will happen to her? She also survives on Gangi's milk!'

Suhagini Devi was infuriated with his remarks. 'Don't utter the name of that nasty bird before me! Ever since she came to our house, inauspicious things are happening' – and she became choked with tears.

Raghu said – 'Why put blame on poor Manavi? She has not done anything evil.'

'OK, OK – she is the doyen of virtues. She just babbles 'Raghu—Raghu' twice or thrice a day and you are prepared to die for her! Is she your kin? There are no crops this year… It is difficult to get fodder for Gangi who is our lifeline. Now she is also gone! It is all because of that bird that bad things are happening….'

Raghu could not tolerate what his mother was speaking, "If Manavi has heard her accusations, how will she feel," he thought and came to the courtyard looking for Manavi. Usually, Manavi stayed near the Tulsi platform. She loved to sleep here.

But she was not here even. Where could she have gone?

'Manavi! Manavi!!' – Raghu called out loudly.

But Manavi did not return his call. Only Golu was calling his mother – 'Ambho! Ambho!'

Raghu's calls echoed around the yard. 'This boy has gone mad after that ghastly bird!' – Suhagini Devi thought and became more morose.

Manavi did not respond to Raghu's call!.' This was unusual.

Was she playing hide and seek with me? But this was not the time to play…Gangi too was missing. Raghu searched for Manavi inside the house. He looked in every nook and corner. But Manavi was nowhere to be seen. He came out and looked around. There was a neem tree in front of the house. Manavi sometimes sat on its branches. No, there was no trace of her even there. Even if it was very dark, the marble white body of Manavi would be easily visible between the green twigs. Maybe she was sitting on the roof. The roof was covered with earthen tiles. If she walked on them, the tiles would be disturbed. Raghu climbed on the neem tree to search on the roof. But Manavi was not there also.

He called again – 'Manavi! Manavi!!'

Seeing him acting like a mad cap, Suhagini Devi became even more distressed. 'When will this boy understand his responsibilities?' – she asked herself.

Raghu searched in the neighborhood. He then went to Sheela's house and asked her if she had seen Manavi. 'Raghu, these birds... they are not to be trusted. She must have flown away!' Sheela said.

No, Manavi cannot go anywhere without informing me– Raghu said to himself loudly.

Ultimately when he was completely exhausted, he felt as if he had lost everything. His eyes were filled with tears. He came to his house and started weeping. Taken by surprise Suhagini Devi rushed to him – 'Why are you weeping?' – she asked.

'Mother! Gangi is gone! Manavi is gone!! We have lost both of them!'

Suhagini Devi embraced him, stroked his head and said—'Don't cry. Gangi cannot remain without Golu and that bird...she cannot remain without you. They will come back. Now take some food.'

Raghu did not eat anything.—' You are crying for a bird? Look, she is unlike us, her association will never be lasting Do not cry for that ordinary bird.' These words of Suhagini Devi did not provide solace to Raghu.

'She is not an ordinary bird, Mother!' – Raghu protested— 'She is Manavi!'

'OK. If you love her so much, she will come back. But we have to search for Gangi tomorrow... We will go to *Kanji-house* and find her out. If Gangi is not to be found, Golu will die and we also...'

'No...no! Golu must not die! We cannot let him die'– Raghu said.

Then sleep overpowered him.

10

It was a dark night. Two hours must have passed. Suddenly Raghu heard Manavi's call – 'Raghu! Raghu!'

He was startled and got up immediately. Manavi was sitting close to him.

'Manavi! where had you gone? I searched for you everywhere!'

'Sh—sh......' Manavi said in a hushed voice – 'Don't shout. Your mother will getup. All day she toils for you! She must get some rest. Raghu, there is some news about Gangi. Come with me.'

Like a mesmerized person, Raghu followed her. They came out in the lane. Manavi sat on the branch of the neem tree.

'Manavi! Where is Gangi? Did you see her?'Raghu asked anxiously.

'Raghu, our Gangi has been captured by some rogues. There were three more cows. When Gangi did not return by the evening, I flew over the village towards the outskirts. Towards the northeast of the outskirts is the farmhouse of Samta Prasad. I saw four men with sticks in their hands driving the cows towards that farmhouse.

I followed them from above. They did not notice me. I heard one of them saying 'Tomorrow these cows will be taken to the slaughterhouse. Nobody in the village will come to know.' I suspect Samta Prasad is behind all this this.'

Samta Prasad wasthe chairman of the Animal Service Society. He ran a *Goshala* and owned a diary. He was known as a cruel man.

'How can it be possible? Samta Prasad claims to be a devotee of cows!'Raghu said.

'Speak in a low voice. I can small danger. Samta Prasad wants that no one should own any cow here, so that everybody in the village buys milk from him. He also sells his cows and oxen to the slaughter house when they stop giving milk. He has a deal with the meat vendors'.

'What should we do then?'

'First we will go to Ishwari Prasad ji's house. He was also searching for his cows all evening and I saw him returning from the pasture just now. Then we will go to Habib Khan's house. Our Gangi, two cows of Ishavari Prasad and one cow of Habib Khan – these four cows are imprisoned in Samta Prasad's farmhouse. We have to act fast without any commotion. Everyone should hold a baton or a nightstick.'

'I must call Sheela also!'

'What will she do?'

'She will tell her father. Her father Sharada Prasad ji is the Principal of our school now. He will help...'

'As far as my understanding goes, that may not be necessary. First, we must go to the houses of Ishwari Prasad ji and Habib Khan ji.'

'Let us do so then, Manavi!'

Raghu rushed to the house of Ishwari Prasad. Flying over and above, Manavi alighted on the roof of Ishwari Prasad. The three-year old son of Ishwari Prasad was crying. He was hungry as he did not get milk in the evening.

'Babuji! Babu ji!!' – Raghu called at the door the house.

Ishwari Prasad came out. – 'You!' – he said – 'What are you doing here on this inauspicious night? Look, I cannot help you, I will not lend you money, I am already upset… there is no milk in the house, my son is crying, he takes only cow's milk in the evening…'

Raghu was panting. He quickly told Ishwari Prasad what Manavi had revealed. Ishwari Prasad immediately took hold of his baton and said – 'I will go to Samata Prasad's farmhouse just now!'

'Don't go alone.' – Manavi warned.

'What does this bird say – did she say anything?' - Ishwari Prasad asked.

"She said, 'Please don't go alone'… goons of Samata Prasad are there. Babuji, we will first go to Habib Khan's house. His cow has also been abducted. Then we will go to Sharada Prasad Sir's house, he will help us."

'Okay.'

Habib Khan was an old man. He listened to what Raghu said, then hurriedly accompanied Raghu and Ishwari Prasad with his two sons. All the five then went to Sharada Prasad's house. He said that he could not come in the night, but he asked two of the school peons to accompany this group.

All of them holding *lathis* and shouting aloud started for the farmhouse of Samata Prasad.

Manavi told Raghu – 'Tell them not to make a noise. They should remain silent and walk quietly. This is a dangerous place. Towards the south of this farmhouse there is a truck standing. All the four cows are captives inside the truck. There is a guard on the main gate. He has a gun with him. There is a rear gate. I have seen that gate. They brought the cows inside from that gate only. The boundary wall is broken at one place in the back, from there one can climb and jump inside. Somebody amongst you should climb the wall and go inside to open the door. It is bolted but not locked.'

Raghu told everybody what Manavi had said. They consulted among themselves and quietly walked towards the back of the farmhouse. Raghu said – 'I will climb the wall and jump inside.'

Habib Khan said – 'No Son, this bird of yours knows everything, she and you should remain with us, my son Rajjab will go inside.'

Rajjab stood on the shoulders of his brother and jumped inside. Then he opened the rear gate. All of them silently trooped in.

What Manavi had said was true. Raghu peeked Gangi there inside the truck. The truck was bolted. One of the peons sent by Sharada Prasad found a ramp to join in the truck and with the help of Ishwari Prasad Raghu unbolted the bolt of the truck. The cows were brought out. Raghu was massaging Gangi. Gangi was responding affectionately with the sound of 'Amba, Amba.' Rajjab and Suleman had hastened out of the place with their father as people in the farmhouse were awakened due the noise of the cows. Someone amongst them spotted these people in the dark and shouted – 'Awake, awake! The village people are carrying away the cows!!

Immediately the manager of the farmhouse rushed there with a pistol in his hand along with two guards holding *lathis*. 'Who are you bloodies and how come you are taking away these cows?' he demanded.

'These are our cows, you have stolen them… Move away, we are taking our cows back.' Ishwari Prasad said.

'Achcha! You will take the cows! I will crush your head and the heads of these people will also be rolling!' – saying this, the man fired a shot from his pistol.

All the men in Raghu's team were terrified. But then suddenly Manavi flew over the head of the man and attacked his head with her beak. 'Oh!'the man cried out. At the same moment, Suleman jumped and attacked him with his *lathi*. Rajjab also rushed to help his brother, but he was attacked by two of the guards of the farmhouse with batons in their hand. Raghu said aloud to the two peons from the school – 'Hey!, why are you standing there like stone ? They are attacking us, you have *lathis*, attack them!'

Ramcharan, one of the peons said – 'We have orders from the Principal Sir not to fight with the farmhouse staff .'

Meanwhile, the man with the pistol fired a shot at Suleman. He was going to fire another shot at Raghu, when Manavi cried - 'Raghu, move away!' The man with the pistol missed his shot. A sharp whistle resounded in the compound at this moment.

'Lo! The police is here!' —Ishwari Prasad cried.

The man with the pistol started running away along with the guards with batons. Rajjab, who had recovered by now, ran after him and hit him on his shoulder with his lathi. The man fell down on the ground. Suleman and Ishwari Prasad ran after the guards.

The police then entered the compound in their Jeep.

11

Dawn was drawing near when Raghu, Gangi and the others reached the village along with Manavi.

Gangi was running towards the house bellowing 'Hamba, Hamba!!' loudly. Golu was also calling her from inside in a miserable voice. Manavi was tired, so she sat on the back of Gangi. Raghu was calling from behind– 'Gangi, Manavi!! Stop! I am also coming!'

Suhagini Devi was perturbed. She had been roaming all over looking desperately for Raghu. —'Where has this boy gone! Hai Bhagwan!', she was mumbling, 'What has happened to my house! No trace of Gangi either. And now Raghu has disappeared! He was sleeping in my lap at night. Seldom does he wake up early. He must have gone to look for that wicked bird… she is also absent since evening…'

And then she saw Gangi running towards her house calling 'Hamba! Hamba!!' loudly. Milk was dripping from her udders.

' Gangi! Where had you been? Poor Golu had been calling you all night! He is very hungry too. And this wicked bird! She has come again!'

At this moment Raghu also appeared. —'Why are you abusing Manavi?', he said, 'Mother! You are always cross with Manavi. It is she who found out our Gangi. In fact, she has saved all of us from a great crisis.'

'Why, what did she do?'

Briefly Raghu told her all that had happened in the night.

'Raghu, I did not know! She is not a bird then but a *devi*, goddess Bhavani incarnate! And I called her... *Hai Ram*!' — Suhagini Devi lamented again and again.

'You are a goddess! Please forgive me', now she apologised.

Manavi was taken aback at this. Raghu said, 'No, don't call her goddess. She will be afraid. Just call her Manavi.'

Suhagini Devi said — 'Manavi! You are really a Manavi! Will you call me Ma?'

Manavi said – 'Ma!'

Suhagini Devi held Manavi in her arms and slowly caressed her feathers.

Next day the news of the police raid at the farmhouse of Samta Prasad appeared in all newspapers. Sharada Prasad, the principal of the village school, was highly praised. It was reported that due to his promptness, the cows of the villagers were rescued; and that it was he who exposed the racket of Samta Prasad. There was no mention of either Raghu or Manavi.

12

From the city of Ullasanagar in Maharashtra, Natraj Circus Company had now moved to Vidisha in Madhya Pradesh. The journey was torturous. The roads were very rough. There were about twenty rabbits with the company; they ran in a circle around the lion in the show. Two of them became ill on the way and died. There were two girls who had the skill to swing in the sky with their legs holding the swing and heads turned down. They too were taken ill.

Somehow Kalanath reached Vidisha. He surveyed the city, met the collector and the police officers and planned for the publicity of his circus by announcing on mike in an auto-rickshaw and advertising in local dailies. The district administration was cooperative. The ground allotted was sufficient. Tents were erected, sweepers were called. Everything was ready within two days.

The circus started on the third day of their arrival. The opening was not very encouraging. Vidisha is a prosperous city, people are simple. But they did not want to spend even a hundred rupee on a circus ticket. They enjoyed the absurd activities of the joker. They were impressed by Maria's performance who rode on a motorcycle in the well of death.

However, not a single ticket priced one thousand rupees for the special class was sold. There were many who wanted passes for this class. To add salt to the injury, the SP ordered that there should be no show on the day of Vijayadashmi falling next week.

'There will be no show tomorrow', —The members of the company were very happy. Julia, Rupa, Sarvesh and others said – 'Let us go on a city tour.'

Kalanath said to himself – 'I do not have any interest in seeing the city. What should I do?'

Suddenly he remembered his last discussion with his elder brother. Almost two months had passed since they had talked to each other. 'Kala! Did you see the India News of today? There is news for you in it...'– Dada had said. At that point, he had read the news about a female swan who has become the beloved of a village boy. After that he had said—'The parrots and *mainas* may utter some words, but people may not be interested in them. We have them in our homes and we can easily make them speak. But if a swan – that a Rajhansa – speaks in the language of human beings, it will be taken as a miracle. You go to that village and somehow buy that swan!'

Should I go and see the swan today? – Kalanath thought. Dada had informed that the village where this miracle was happening was close to Vidisha, but he has forgotten the name of the village, 'Did I write about my discussion with Dada that day in my diary? Let me see.'

Kalanath did not write diary daily. Occasionally he felt like writing about his impressions and experiences in his diary before going to sleep or after getting up early in the morning. 'Perhaps I did write about my discussion with Dada that day before going to sleep' – he said to himself and took out his diary from his suitcase. Turning over the pages of the diary he found this entry dated 11.8.1990. It was like this—

"After a long time today in the morning I had a discussion with Dada. It was a delight talking to him. I have been feeling lonely all these days…I have no family, no home. This circus company is my family, and its camp my home. Still, I long for my relatives…When I met Bhabhi and Dada in Delhi last month, I was overwhelmed with joy. Then they came to see my show. Dada is now reconciled with me. And Bhabhi! She loves me!…Dada read out a news published in a daily for me. It was about village Nandanpur of Vidisha district. There a female swan has become intimate with a ten-year-old boy called Raghu. She talks to this boy. She even speaks like human beings. Dada had advised me to go to Nandanpur and buy that swan. I promised him, I would do so…"

Kalanath closed the diary, "So Nandanpur is the name of the village where that miracle happened, and the village was very close to this city – he told himself. Let me ask Ramsevak if he knows anything about this village and the swan which talks like human beings."

Ramsevak lived in Vidisha. He himself had met Kalanath to enquire if there was any job for him in the circus. He was a good fellow. He did whatever he was asked to do. Kalanath entrusted him with the job of supplying grocery and vegetables for the mess in his company. Earlier, the cook in the mess himself would go to the market and purchase the goods needed by him. Ramsevak was a good helper. Sugarcane for the elephants were to be brought, meat for the lion, green grass for the rabbits – all these things he would supply. Ramsevak was an honest man. He was satisfied with the allowance of fifty rupees per day which Kalanath gave him. Kalanath was now dependent upon him for many services. You do not get such a dutiful servant so cheap in other cities.

It was going to be nine o'clock. Ramsevak usually came at this hour. Kalanath was eagerly awaiting.

'Namaste. Sahib!'

'Oh, Ramsevak? You will live long…I was just remembering you!'

At this Ramsevak started laughing – Ho...Ho…Ho…

Kalanath was pleased with his laughter. – 'Did you bring sugarcane for the elephants? And what did you do for the food of the rabbits? Yesterday I asked you to bring gram for the horse?'

'Everything has been arranged for, Sahib. No worries.'

'No worries' was the pet phrase of Ramsevak.

'Why should I not worry, Ramsevak! You do not know perhaps that two of my rabbits died on the way to Vidisha… there is only one horse with us and he too seems ill. The climate of this place does not suit him…If he does not cross three hurdles in the show ..one of my items will be spoiled.'

'Nothing will be spoiled, Sahib! No worries'

'Ramsevak! you speak as if you know everything. Do you know where Nandanpur is?'

'Nandanpur? Of course Sahib, I know Nandanpur very well! My sister lives there!'

'Your sisters are spread all around world, it seems! You call all the girls of our circus 'Bahen ji'. All the young ladies of Vidisha are your sisters. You fool! How will you marry if you regard all ladies as your sisters? OK, do you know about a talking swan in Nandanpur?'

'No Sahib! I do not know of any swan. Do you have any work at Nandanpur?'

'There is a boy named Raghu there…I want to meet him.'

'Ho-Ho…No worries, Sahib! Raghu is my nephew!'

'Achcha! Now you have a nephew also! Ramsevak! You tell a lot of lies!'

'No, Sahib! I am telling you the truth. See Sahib, Suhagini Devi is the mother of Raghu and she is my real sister. Therefore, Raghu is my nephew.'

'OK, can we go to Nandanpur just now and return by afternoon?'

'No, Sahib! There is only one bus plying to Nandapur and that runs in the afternoon. After that there is no bus in the evening to return from there.'

'You fool! We will go by car!'

'By car? Ho-Ho! No worries, Sahib! We go from here and return in an hour from there!'

'Let us go then!'

'When shall we go Sahib?'

'You fool! We will go immediately, and you are coming with me to Nandanpur because Raghu, your nephew, is there. You shall introduce me to him.'

'No, Sahib! I cannot go immediately.'

'Why not?'

'Sahib....my elder sister is there. She is Raghu's mother. Her name, I told you, is Suhagini Devi.'

'You fool! What is the problem if she is there?'

'Problem is there, Sahib! My sister lives in Nandanpur! If I go to Nandanpur with you, I will also meet her. To meet her, I will have to go to her house. If I go to her house, I must carry a sari. And some sweets also for my nephew. Otherwise, what sort of brother am I? I had no money, Sahib on of Rakshabandhan this year...not even for bus fare! So I could not go to my sister for getting the rakhi tied on my wrist.'

Saying this, Ramsevak's eyes welled with tears. Kalanath was moved. He stood up from his armchair and patted Ramsevak on his back. —'Oh, Ramsevak! You are a man! Don't cry like a child! You tell everybody 'Not to worry' and you are worrying yourself. You should be happy that you will be meeting your sister and your nephew and giving them gifts!'

'Ho-Ho Sahib! I am very happy. I am weeping because I am happy. You just wait for one hour, Sahib. I will go to the market and purchase a sari and some sweets. Then we can go. There I go and here I come!'

'There is no time, Ramsevak! There is no show today, but I have lots of work to do...we will just start from here to purchase a sari for your sister and something for your nephew on the way.'

'Ho-Ho, Sahib. That is fine, Sahib!'

Ramsevak was delighted. He could not go to meet his sister on the occasion of Rakshabandhan this year. She must have been waiting…and when he did not reach Nandanpur that day, she must have felt very bad…Now she will be happy to see him.

Seated in the car with Ramsevak, Kalanath asked the driver to go through the market. Ramsevak was going to purchase a cheap sari. Kalanath reprimanded him – 'Ramsevak! You are going to meet your sister after a long time, you should purchase a good sari. You also purchase some garments for your nephew, Raghu. Don't bother about the payment. I will pay for everything.'

Ramsevak was embarrassed. 'Why has this sahib has become so generous all of a sudden?' he thought—'Today he is paying for the purchases, and tomorrow he will deduct all the money from my wages, what will I do then?'

13

It was noon when Kalanath and Ramsevak reached Nandanpur. Though autumn had gone by, still the sun was very hot. The lane in which Raghu lived was narrow. 'Car will not go inside,'the driver said.

Ramsevak protested vehemently—'Oh, what are you talking? I know that cars can go right up to my sister's house. Tractors used to pass through this *gali*...'

Saying this, he became emotional. When his brother-in-law was alive, tractors with trolley full of crops used to come here.

Finally he got down from the car and rushed towards the house of his sister, calling—'Raghu! Raghu!'

His call was returned by a soft twinkling voice – 'Raghu! Raghu!!'

Ramsevak was startled. 'What a strange sound!', he said— 'I never seem to have heard this sound. Seems as if a two-year child is speaking. But Raghu does not have a younger sister!'

He again called – 'Raghu, Raghu!!'

The same sound came again from the house – 'Raghu! Raghu!!'

Ramsevak was irritated now. He shouted – 'O you, child! I am calling for Raghu! Why are you teasing me?'

Meanwhile Kalanath had come behind him. He put his hand on his shoulder and said – 'Sh..sh! don't shout! I think it is Manavi talking.'

'Manavi? How do you know, Sahib, that some girl called Manavi lives in this house? This didi of mine! She is always showing some girl or the other to me. I am never going to marry…!'

Kalanath was fed up with him. He asked Ramsevak to keep quiet and called out- 'Is Raghu there?'

Suhagini Devi responded from within the house – 'No, Raghu is not in the house!'

The same voice like the chirping of a bird repeated –'Raghu is not in the house! Raghu is not in the house!!'

Kalanath was thrilled. The news which Dada had read out to him from some newspaper was true then! The bird speaks so clearly like a human being!

'Didi! It is I – Rammu!' – Ramsevak said aloud. 'Who is this child repeating every word like a parrot?'

Suhagini Devi rushed. Seeing Ramsevak she exclaimed – 'Oh Rammu Bhaiya! You!' And she started weeping. Ramsevak touched her feet and also started weeping. Then in a choked voice he introduced Kalanath – 'Didi, this is my Sahib…He is a great Sahib! He runs a circus company! I am in his service these days. Whatever he pays, that helps me sail through.'

Suhagini Devi said 'Namaste' to Kalanath with folded hands. Kalanath came forward and touched her feet. Suhagini Devi remarked with embarrassment –'What are you doing Sahib? You are Rammu's Sahib!'

Kalanath laughed and said, 'You are the elder sister of Ramsevak, so you are my sister also, and a sister is always to be respected.'

Saying this he again laughed with a gurgling sound.

Ramsevak was astounded. 'How come this sahib has changed so much all of a sudden?' – he thought – 'He is behaving in a strange way. But if he is laughing, shall I laugh too?' Thinking this, he also started laughing with a gurgling sound. Kalanath eyed him sharply, and Ramsevak was stopped.

At this moment, Raghu came back from school. He was delighted to see Ramsevak and said beamingly – 'Oh Mamaji! When did you come? What did you bring for me? Why did you not come on Rakhi this year? Mother was waiting for you all day long!'

Sahagini Devi rebuked her son –'Mama has come after a long time and you are tormenting him with your complaints! Go and fetch water for him…and for his Sahib also!'

'So this is the boy who figured in the news item read out to me by Dada', Kalanath thought – 'He is the lover of that female swan. I will have to woo him. Only he can rescue my circus from the crisis…'

Thinking this he went to the car and took out the garments purchased for Raghu. Handing them over to him he said—'Raghu, my son! Here is a shirt and some trousers for you.'

Meanwhile, Raghu had brought two glasses of water. 'For me?' —he was startled—'Who are you? Who brought these garments?'

Ramsevak said with enthusiasm—'Raghu, he is my Sahib. He is a great man. He runs a great circus company.'

Looking at Kalanath in amazement, Raghu said—'You run a circus company? I want to see circus. Sheela went to Vidisha last week. She saw circus there. There is a lion in the circus—she said. I want to see the lion too.'

'You will see everything'—Kalanath said—'We can go today itself, why delay?'

At this moment Manavi came out and said—'Raghu has come! Raghu has come!!'—Then flying over them she sat on a branch of the neem tree.

Raghu rushed to her and said—'Manavi, come down! We will play.'

Manavi was somehow afraid of Kalanath and Ramsevak, She said—'No, I will not come down.'

Kalanath was watching Manavi and his eyes were wide open with wonder. He could not make out what she had just said. 'So, she is that swan!' —he said to himself—'She speaks clearly...If Raghu joins my circus, one item of the lady swan in love with this boy can be added. But they both need training. We will have to depict them as two lovers of past lives. Raghu will ask her in the show—'Will you marry me, my fair lady? She will first reject his proposal and then slowly she will agree. The dialogues should be framed in a proper language ... Ravindra who plays a joker in my circus will do that .. he is good at writing dialogues. We will announce like this–'See the story of immortal love ... love never dies.'

In his reverie he suddenly thought of Vandana. Does she still love me? No. I must not think about her.

Coming out of his world of dreams, he asked Suhagini Devi—"Sister if you allow, we will take Raghu and this bird to show them circus... you can also come…"

'First you come inside and have some refreshments.'—Suhagini Devi said.

Kalanath was not interested in staying too long. 'We should leave this place as early as possible.' he whispered in Ramsevak's ears—'We can take Raghu and your sister to Vidisha, tell them to get ready immediately.'

Ramsevak said aloud—'Didi, Sahib is very busy, he is in a hurry. We have come here to take you and Raghu to Vidisha…get ready soon.'

Suhagini Devi had gone to the kitchen. She was just lighting the *chulha*. Daily she brought pieces of dry branches and wood from the nearby jungle to use as fuel.

Smoke came out when the chulha was kindled. Kalanath started coughing with the sound of Khoh—khoh—

Seeing this Ramsevak shouted again — 'Didi, what are you doing! Sahib is feeling uneasy because of the smoke.'

'OK, but tea is ready!' —saying this, Suhagin Devi came with two mugs of tea. Kalanath's attention was focused on Raghu and Manavi. He could see from the door how Raghu was playing with Manavi. He was running and jumping all over the ground to catch Manavi who was flying above his head. He was also talking to her. Kalanath tried to listen to what Manavi was saying. He could hear only two words – No, no!!

Suhagini Devi sat on the ground talking to him. He was asking her to come to Vidisha. Suhagini Devi was saying – 'How can I go to Vidisha? You take Raghu for one day. I have to look after a mother, a daughter and two sons!'

'What are you saying?' – Ramsevak was amazed – 'There is nobody in the house except you and Raghu. Our mother died years ago…From where did this mother, daughter and two sons come? Raghu is the only nephew I have…'

Suhagini Devi said – 'See Rammu, Gangi is here. She is my mother. She gives us her milk like a mother. And her calf … Golu. He is my little son. He is only three months old. And then Manavi… she is my daughter., You know she calls me Mother.'

'Who is Manavi? How do you become her mother?'

'Ramsevak! Perhaps you did not see Manavi? Raghu is playing with her outside.'

Kalanath remonstrated.

'Ho, ho…that bird…you call her Manavi? What a name! Who gave her this name?'

'She herself told me her name is Manavi.'

Suddenly they heard Manavi speaking in a sharp tone – 'No. No, I am not going!'

Kalanath's eyes were fixed on Manavi all the time. Seeing him so interested in the bird, Ramsevak asked him – 'Sahib, shall I ask Raghu to come here with that bird?'

'Yes, yes!' Kalanath said, 'I see that Raghu loves that bird! If he is coming to Vidisha, that bird can come along with him too!'

Ramsevak called Raghu. He came in, holding Manavi in his hands. 'Raghu! Sahib asks you to get ready to accompany him to Vidisha! We are leaving.'

Raghu said – 'No! I am not coming to Vidisha with you!'

Kalanath was shocked to hear this. 'Why not? he asked – 'you just said that you will come with us! You can see circus there!'

'Manavi says she will not come, and I cannot leave her alone.'

'What is the problem with her? Why is she afraid? She can travel comfortably with us in the car.' Kalanath said.

'Poor Manavi…she thinks that the swans of her group may come to this village any day. The swans have not come here in this season so far and the season is ending…I read the statement of the great ornithologist Salim Ali. He says that due to pollution in this area, swans will not come from the Himalayas here, they have gone to Bharatpur.'

'Our circus is going to Bharatpur next month, half of the month is already over. We will go to Bharatpur just after ten days for our next show. I can take you and Manavi to Bharatpur'

'Manavi! What do you say? Sahib will take us to Bharatpur. Are you then willing to come?'

Manavi did not reply. She was still afraid of Kalanath. She suspected his intentions. Raghu again said – 'Manavi, what do you say?'

'As you wish' - finally Manavi said in a weak voice which only Raghu could hear.

Kalanath was curious. He asked - 'What did she say? Did she say something?'

'Manavi will come with us to Vidisha,' Raghu said jubilantly and started dancing.

Suhagini Devi's eyes welled with tears. She told Raghu – 'See that nobody touches Manavi. She should not fly on her own. You should always hold her in your hands!'

Ramsevak was startled.'So much love for a bird!' – he wondered.

'I promise, I will do that! ' – Raghu said.

'I will do that! I will do that!' – Manavi repeated after him.

Suhagini Devi instructed Raghu in a harsher tone – 'Don't do any mischief at Vidisha. Always be in Mama's company. And don't trouble him.'

'I will not trouble Mama. I promise.'

Suhagini Devi softly caressed Manavi on her back and said – 'Come back to Nandanpur soon. OK?'

'OK' – Manavi said.

Then Suhagini Devi told Ramsevak – 'Rammu, Raghu is very naughty. Don't allow him to go anywhere on his own. He should not go near the cages of the lion and bears. And see that he comes back here tomorrow.'

'No worries, Didi! I will myself drop him tomorrow to Nandanpur' – Ramsevak said and touched his sister's feet. Kalanath also bowed down before her. Suhagini Devi came out to see them off. Raghu got into the car holding Manavi.

14

Kalanath sat on the front seat with the driver. Ramsevak was lulled into sleep as soon as the car reached the outskirts of Nandanpur. Manavi still appeared sad. She was missing Suhagini Devi. Mother is as pure hearted as her son Raghu is – she thought, 'Shall I return to her and Raghu from Vidisha or will I be able to join my group at Bharatapur? – She was in a dilemma.'

Ramsevak wanted to take Raghu to his house as soon as they reached Vidisha. Kalanath said – 'Ramsevak, your house is in a very narrow lane and a dirty drainage flows across that lane. Manavi will faint because of the foul smell there. Raghu, what do you say, will it be right if you stay in our camp with Manavi? It is quite neat and clean there.'

Raghu has once been to the house of his Mama and had not liked its surroundings. He was also curious to see life in a circus camp. So he said – 'I think I will stay in the camp with Manavi…Manavi faints even at the breath of people!'

'So this is settled then. Raghu and Manavi will stay in a tent house in our camp. OK, Ramsevak Bhai?'

Ramsevak was a little shocked. But he was touched by Kalanath addressing him as 'bhai'. In a feeble voice he said – 'Let it be so, Sahib!'

'OK, some goods are to be brought from the market. You take my vehicle and bring those items. Hurry up!' – saying this, Kalanath handed him a slip of paper.

Ramsevak glanced at the list of items on the slip – two kilos of black gram, one quintal wheat flour…twenty sugar canes…

'Ramsevak, hurry! Otherwise we will not be able to feed the elephants and the horse today…'

'Shall I take Raghu with me, Sahib?' – Ramsevak asked.

'Don't worry about Raghu. I will be with him. Let him settle down here first.'

'Raghu! I am just coming.' - Ramsevak told Raghu in a feeble voice and departed.

Kalanath showed Raghu a tent house. – 'This house is reserved for VIPs. This will be yours and Manavi's residence now.'

Raghu was curiously eying the arrangement inside the tent house. One big palanquin, a table and a chair, a wash basin…..'

Then Kalanath called out at the next tent house – 'Ravindra! Ravindra!!'

A young man came out. 'Babuji! When did you come back? You had gone to some village to bring some bird…' he said.

'Sh—Sh...' Kalanath stopped him before he could complete his sentence. Then he talked to him in some strange language. Ravindra was nodding and saying – 'Yes, Babuji, yes, Babuji!!'

Then Kalanath called Raghu. – 'Raghu! I will introduce you to Ravindra', he said, 'He is like your elder brother. You can call him Ravi Dada. He will show you our camp here. Tomorrow we start the show in the afternoon. You will be our special guest there. You keep a watch over Manavi. Don't leave her company…there are dangerous animals in our circus. She should not be allowed to fly alone. The monkeys may do her harm.'

Raghu enjoyed the tour around the camp. Everybody called Kalanath 'Babuji'.

Roaming in the camp he was able to see the animals in the cages. He was holding Manavi in his hands. Manavi looked serious and sometimes she appeared to have gone to sleep. At one place the bear trainer was making the bear dance and at another place three monkeys – one couple with a baby were playing. They were tied to a tree with a rope. They also saw the grand elephant. He was called Airawat. The company had three elephants, Airawat was the biggest among them. Raghu's eyes widened at his large white tusks. They were as white as Manavi.

After a while Babuji left them. Ravindra was continuously chatting with Raghu and describing the sights. He was very attentive towards Manavi and tried to listen carefully whenever Manavi spoke.

'Dada, do you also perform in the show?' – Raghu asked Ravindra.

'I am the joker of this circus,' Ravindra said.

'Joker? But you do not look like a joker!' Raghu said, surprised.

'When I play the joker, I look like a joker' – Ravindra said. 'You will see me in my attire tomorrow.'

They turned towards the lady's wing. –'How do I look Raghu, if I do not look like a joker?'Ravindra asked.

'You appear to be a nice gentlemen.'

'Persons who play joker in the circus are all nice gentlemen, Raghu! Those who appear nice gentlemen in actual life may be real jokers.'

Raghu could not understand what he was saying. But he liked Ravindra's company. Ravindra told him about his life. He belonged to Kolkata. 'I have studied up to B.A. I was a good student. I passed all examinations in first division. Then I became a teacher in a school. I wanted to study further, but then I joined this circus company', he said.

'You are a highly educated person. How come you are serving as a joker in this circus company?' Raghu asked.

Before Ravindra could reply to him, a young lady coming out from the ladies' wing approached him and waving her hands said – 'Hello, dear!' After that Ravindra started talking to her in a strange language. It was the same language in which Kalanath was talking to Ravindra earlier today.

The lady was of very fair color, tall and attractive. Her voice was as melodious as that of Manavi', but the words she uttered could be heard very clearly.

'Oh! I did not introduce you to our guest!' – suddenly Ravindra spoke in Hindi – 'He is Raghu. He joined us today. And she is Manavi, – his companion, the lady swan!'

'Oh...ho – What a pleasure!' – the lady said – 'So this is that smart chap – Raghu! So cute!'

Raghu was blushing. – 'Look! How he is blushing like a girl!', the lady said and laughed aloud.

Ravindra was smiling. He told Raghu – 'This is Maria. You were asking why I joined this circus. She is the reason behind it. I joined this circus because of her.'

Raghu could not understand what he was saying.

'OK I am going to inspect the death well. Some beams there are broken. It needs repairing. OK Raghu, see you later… you are going to be with us now!'

Saying this, Maria hurriedly departed. Raghu was surprised by her remark. He asked Ravindra—'Why did she say that? I am here only for one day. I will go back to Nandanpur tomorrow. My mother is waiting for me … and Manavi…she does not seem to be liking this place.'

'She said something jocularly. Don't take it seriously.'

The place where this circus company was camped was called Ramlila Maidan. It was a huge ground. There seemed to be hundreds of tents set up there. The animals were all lodged separately. Taking a round with Ravindra in the ground, Raghu was tired. Manavi also appeared sleepy. It was evening. Raghu said – 'I feel hungry.'

'OK, let us have some food.'

Ravindra said, 'There is kitchen and a mess in the northeast corner of the ground. They entered a big tent. There were about fifty chairs with tables there. Ravindra said- 'You sit here with Manavi. I will see what they have in the kitchen.'

After a while, the raised voice of the chef from the kitchen could be heard – 'Oh, nobody eats here on time. Some have taken their lunch just now. Dinner time today starts at seven-thirty. Babu ji has announced already. And it is five-thirty already.'

Ravindra was speaking in a hushed tone, so Raghu could not hear what he was saying. But after five minutes, Raghu saw him returning with a waiter who was holding a plate in his hand. He placed the plate before Raghu on the table. It contained rice and lentil.

"Raghu, take this today. Tomorrow we will have a grand breakfast."

'What about you? Why don't you eat with us?' – Raghu asked

Ravindra laughed and said – 'I will have dinner after some time. You have met Maria…I will have dinner with her.'

'What about Manavi?'

'What about her?'

'She also needs to be fed.'

'O yes! We have to feed her too. I will see what is there for her.'

A waiter came with a jug full of water and a glass and he placed the jug and the glass on the table before Raghu.

'Bring something for this swan.' – Ravindra told him.

'For this bird?' waiter said– 'No, we don't have anything for her here. Take her to the animal's mess. There they might be having some grass or grains.'

'No! Manavi is not going there…She does not take grass or grains...if there is nothing here for her, then I will also not eat anything!' – Raghu said in an agitated voice and pushed aside his plate of food.

'Don't be angry, Raghu!' – Ravindra said patting Raghu's back –'Everything will be arranged for Manavi. She is our VIP guest!'

Ravindra then put his hand on the waiter's shoulder and went out with him. After five minutes the waiter came back holding a plate with some leaves of spinach and a mug full of milk. He placed the plate and the mug before Raghu.

Raghu said – 'Manavi! Now take something.'

'I do not feel like eating anything, Raghu! You have your dinner!' – Manavi said.

'Wonderful!' – Ravindra exclaimed – 'She talks so clearly! There are seven wonders of the world, this is the eighth one.'

'See Manavi! How Ravindra Dada is praising you. Now take something.' – Caressing her feathers Raghu pleaded again.

Sitting with knees on the ground, Ravindra bowed before Manavi and entreated – 'Madam, Madam! This is my request. Please have something!'

Raghu was laughing at this theatrical act.

Persistently requested by Raghu and Ravindra, Manavi reluctantly picked up some spinach leave.

Neither Raghu nor Manavi could sleep properly that night. Early in the morning they were aroused by the dreadful roar of the lion.

‘Manavi, I am not feeling good here. I do not know where Rammu Mama has vanished. I think he is angry with me because we did not stay in his house. But Babuji asked us to stay here for our comfort.

‘Everybody pursues his own self -interest.’ – Manavi said, grumblingly.

‘What self-interest? What are you saying?’ Raghu was surprised by her tone.

‘Nothing. It was not proper for you to leave your mother alone in the village’

‘Today we will see the circus show in the afternoon and return to Nandanpur. But then – what will happen to you trip to Bharatpur? The members of your group may be coming to Bharatpur sanctuary.’

Manavi looked at Raghu gravely and said – ‘It seems that the members of my group have forgotten me… They may not come to Bharatpur.’

In the evening, Kalanath visited the tent house of Raghu thrice to enquire if he and Manavi needed anything. ‘I have made special arrangements for cow’s milk for Manavi’ – he told Raghu. Manavi felt more comfortable now as she sipped some milk. Ravindra was constantly keeping a watch to make their stay comfortable. As his tent was adjacent to theirs, Raghu could even call him from his tent.

15

The first show of the circus next day started in the afternoon at three. Raghu and Manavi were seated in the front row reserved for VIPs. The adjacent seats on both sides were vacant, Kalanath and Ravindra occasionally came and occupied them. Raghu did not first recognize Ravindra in the joker's attire. He had a triangular colorful cap on his head and was wearing loose pajamas and a shirt with several colorful strips. The tip of his nose and cheeks were painted red. He really could make the viewer's laugh by his awkward movements and stupid remarks. Raghu was amused at this transformation of Ravindra.

The first item presented a parade of the all the artists of the company. It was a spectacular sight. Gradually they departed with rhythmic movements and a group of ten girls remained. Two girls climbed over the shoulders of three, and one climbed on the shoulders of two. Then the remaining two girls stood on the knees of the two girls on the sides in the first row, holding the hands of the two girls in the second row above. The remaining two girls started doing acrobatics. Bending backwards they inserted their heads out of their feet.

Ravindra awkwardly tried to hold the remaining two girls on his knees, holding each of their hands. In his attempt he deliberately fell down. The audience laughed.

'Manavi, do you see – what a wonderful sight!' – Raghu said.

Suddenly there was an accident. The girl standing on the shoulders of the two girls on the top of this human mountain was unsettled and fell down on the ground. Ravindra was alert, he picked up that girl immediately and ran inside. Dismantling the structure, the remaining girls also ran inside.

Kalanath put his hand on Raghu's shoulder and said – 'Raghu, please help us! You go in the ring and call Manavi! Manavi will fly to you! After that Ravidnra will manage everything!'

Raghu could not get him. Kalanath almost snatched Manavi from his hands. Ravindra had now come back in the ring and was announcing on the mike – 'We are going to show you a wonderful love story. Love between a female swan and a boy Raghu! This is a story of love lasting several lives. Raghu is her lover. Where is Raghu? Raghu, are you coming?'

'Raghu, go to Ravindra!' Kalanath urged Raghu.

Raghu rose and went where Ravindra was standing. Ravindra asked him on the mike –'Hello dear! Where is your sweetheart? Can you call her? Please call her!'

Raghu called aloud – 'Manavi! Manavi!!'

Ravidnra held the mike before his mouth. The audience became expectant.

At this moment Kalanath released Manavi. She flew towards the ring and made rounds above Raghu's head.

'See, that white bird! She is playing with that boy!'– Some children in the audience cried out.

Making circles vertically and horizontally over Raghu like a dancer, Manavi finally sat on his shoulder. Children in the audience were clapping.

Ravindra acting as a joker tried to hold her in his hands, Manavi flew away from him. Ravindra told Raghu – 'Please ask her to sit in your lap!'

Manavi sat on the arms of Raghu. Ravindra asked her – 'Manavi! Will you marry me?'

Manavi said – 'No. no!!'

The audience cried out in glee– 'Oh, it's a speaking bird !'

Ravindra started weeping in a mocking way and said– 'Uuuuh! She has rejected me! She loves Raghu!'

The children were now laughing aloud. Some of them were rolling in the ground with their hands on their belly.

Raghu joined the play. He told Manavi – 'Manavi, he is weeping. Tell him not to weep.'

Manavi raised her beak and facing Ravindra she said – 'Don't weep. You will also get married….'

Ravindra was astonished. Married? I? Oh? But with whom?

'With some girl, of course!', – Manavi said.

'But I want you, my fair lady!'

'No, you don't want me. You want Maria!', Manavi said.

The audience was amazed at Manavi's performance. 'Look, how clearly that bird speaks! I think, he is a Rishi!' - A man in the audience remarked.

His wife immediately intercepted – 'Not he! She is a female. Therefore she has wisdom!'

At this moment Kalanath joined the ring and gave a signal to Ravindra that Maria was ready for her performance. Putting his hand on Raghu's shoulder, Ravindra said – 'OK Raghu, thanks a lot! We return to our seats!'

Taking a backward step towards the VIPs seats, dramatically he started dancing before Manavi and said – 'Please come this way!'

Holding the mike, Kalanath was announcing – 'Now we come to the most challenging part of our item. Maria will drive her motor cycle in the death well. See how the lady faces death face to face…'

By this time, Ravindra had brought Raghu and Manavi back to their seats. Raghu was dazzled and nervous. He was trembling. His heart was thumping. He could not assess how all this could happen.

Ravindra has gone to the ring again and he was dancing, jumping and making circular turns on his back.

'Manavi, I am unable to understand how all this happened.'– Raghu was telling Manavi.

'I knew that something like this would happen…' Manavi said slowly.

'You knew? How did you know?'

'Raghu! You are too simple. This Circus company is a trap. Now you are caught in it…They will not let us go back… neither me nor you.'

'What are you saying! We are going back to Nandanpur tomorrow.'

Before Manavi could say anything, Kalanath joined them. Sitting beside Raghu and caressing his back, he said in a pleasing tone – 'That was wonderful! Raghu, you will become a great artist one day. Our audience is simply charmed by Manavi. Actually, you both have saved us from a great crisis. You saw for yourself how in accident one of the girls on the human pyramid fell down. Maria's item was to follow, but she was not ready. She said – she will take ten minutes. So I told Ravindra, 'Our Raghu is a great artist!' So is Manavi! She is simply superb! I have no words to express my thanks to you two...'

'Raghu, ask him how that girl who had fallen down.' Manavi said.

Raghu repeated what she was saying.

Kalanath said – 'O! that girl! She will be OK. She has some injury in her head! It's not very serious. We have three doctors in our company. One of them is a vetenary doctor, the other one is a lady doctor and the third one a general physician. Dressing has been done on the wound of that girl. Sometimes such accidents happen. The audience does not even know that something has happened. Because you both were seated in the first row for VIPs, you had a close view and could see what had happened.'

That very moment a person came and told Kalanath – 'Babuji, Airawat is not well…he is refusing to come out…'

'OK, I am coming,' Kalanath said and left with him.

Raghu remembered Airawat – the big elephant with huge white tusks. Maria's running the motorcycle in death well was over in two or three minutes. The audience remained wonderstruck during these minutes. Then there was the item of walking on the rope. Roli and Shankari gave the performance. Their father Satyadev was present to assist them. Satyadev belonged to the Banjara community of Rajasthan.

A rope of fifty feet length was tied on the two columns. Roli climbed on the column from one side and started walking on the rope. Shankari did the same from the other side. They met at the middle point. Roli raised Shankari and held her on her knees. Then they changed directions. Roli placed Shankari in the direction she had come from and she returned the way Shankari had come from. This skill must have been very tough to master.

After this there was the show of rabbits and lion. Raghu was feeling tired now. Manavi was not even seeing what was going in the ring. She had gone in a trance with her eyes shut.

Raghu asked her, 'Manavi, are you OK? You do not want to see the rest of the show?'

'No, Raghu!'Manavi said. 'We better go to our tent house.'

Raghu got up to go. Ravindra immediately rushed towards them and asked – 'What happened, Raghu? Are you leaving?'

'Manavi wants to rest.'

'Oh sure! She must be tired. There are some interesting items remaining though. But you can see them in the night show. Babuji is very happy with the performance of you both in this show. It seems we will again require your help in the night show...You know Airawat, he is not well...'

Ravindra accompanied them to their tent. He stopped on the doorway and asked – 'Shall I send you something to eat? You must be hungry?'

'I do not feel like eating anything. I had enough lunch. It will be good if some milk is available for Manavi.'

'OK, I will arrange for milk. Raghu, you can also take some milk. Take rest. You can come and sit in the balcony for the evening show. You will enjoy it better as there will be lights. Otherwise, I will come to take you when your presence is required.'

After ten minutes, a waiter came and placed two glasses of milk on the table before Raghu. Manavi was not willing to have the milk. Raghu insisted that she should sip a little. Somehow Manavi took a quarter glass of the milk. Raghu started drinking the remaining milk. After the first sip his eyebrows narrowed and he said – 'It is tasting foul, not the least like the milk of our Gangi!'

They tried to take some rest. The ground was lit up with street bulbs. Raghu put out the light in their tent.

Raghu soon fell into a slumber and was seeing his mother in his dream. He was shaken out of sleep when Ravindra called and told Raghu that he and Manavi were again needed for their performance in the next show. Raghu reluctantly went with Manavi. It went on well. The audience was delighted and there was a thunderous applause at Manavi's remarks.

After his performance with Manavi, Raghu immediately came back to his tent. He firmly told Kalanath and Ravindra—'I have seen enough of circus. We will be going back early in the morning to Nandanpur. Please arrange for our departure!'

He could not sleep properly that night. It was for the first time in his life that he was away from his mother. The memories of his mother were haunting him. Then he remembered Rammu Mama. Where had he vanished? I should have asked him before presenting the item in the circus. He must be very angry with me for this. He does not like Manavi…But considering that mother had instructed him to take care of Manavi and me, he should have come to see us.

'Manavi! Are you awake?' – he asked Manavi.

'Yes.' - Manavi whispered.

'Manavi, why did you say that this circus company is a trap and we are caught in it? And how is it that this fellow – Babuji -- will not allow us to leave this place?'

'Why did he come to Nandanpur and why was he insisting so much on our coming to Vidisha? In your society, nobody does anything without a selfish motive.'

Raghu was surprised and shocked. He said – 'Manavi, really…I did not think that way.'

'You did not think that way because you are a person with a pure heart. Others are not like that. Be careful tomorrow. Kalanath ji will use all his tricks to prolong our stay here. OK., now go to sleep. We will talk about it tomorrow.'

16

Manavi was right. Early in the morning next day, Kalanath, or Babuji as he was called here,visited Raghu's tent. He was trying to do all sorts of things to please Raghu. _'Raghu, what will you have for breakfast today? We can have halva and jalebi and poha also…and what about Manavi? What does she like?'

'Actually Babuji, it is very kind of you to provide all this hospitability to us…but my mother is alone at Nandanpur. I have to help her in many household responsibilities… so, as we had decided earlier, we both would like to go back.'

Kalanath was taken aback with this plain declaration. But immediately he became normal and said in a cool voice – 'Oh sure.. I will arrange for a vehicle for you to go to Nandanpur. Thank you very much, Raghu! You have been so helpful. Also, please keep this…'-

Saying this he thrust one hundred rupee note in Raghu's pocket.

'Why are to giving this to me? No,no, I cannot take it.'

'I am also your Mama like Rammu Mama. Take this from your Mama! And please don't go without breakfast.

I have asked Ramsevak, your Mamaji, I mean to bring special items of your taste for your breakfast.'

As he was saying this, Ramsevak appeared on the scene. 'Rammu Mama! where did you disappear? You did not see our show also in the circus!' – Raghu chided him.

'I was there. I saw your show – Manavi's show actually – Ramsevak said – 'I was sitting in the back row…I saw you both in both the shows yesterday …I have brought Jalebi and Poha for you.'

'And for Manavi?'

'I have brought cow's milk for her.' – Ramsevak said.

Breakfast was served. Manavi sipped some milk. Babu ji insisted that Ramsevak should have his breakfast with them. All the time during the breakfast, he was talking to Raghu – asking questions about his education, his food habits, hobbies, etc. Raghu was telling him that he wanted to be fluent in English. Kalanath said with enthusiasm – 'Don't worry! We can make you as expert in conversational English! Our Ravindra is here. He was a teacher of English at Kolkata! He has trained several boys and girls of our company who now talk fluently in English. But you will have to stay here for seven days for that!'

Raghu was surprised. 'In seven days! Our English teacher Sharma Sir tells us that we are fools and we will not be able to learn English even if we devote our whole life to it.'

'Your Sharma Sir is himself a fool!' – Babuji said and laughed – ho- ho ho!!!

There was winter vacation in the school from tomorrow. Raghu was in a fix. If he stayed here for seven days and

Ravidnra Dada taught him, he world speak English fluently, 'When I return back to Nandanpur, everybody will be surprised to see me speaking English…'

But soon he was nailed down by the memories of Nandanpur, 'What must mother be doing at this hour? Daily she would get up early in the morning and place a pan full of grass before Gangi. Then Golu will be released to suck milk.'

Today mother must have milked Gangi herself. Since Raghu had learnt how to milk Gangi, he had been doing this job for the past few months.

'What are you thinking, Raghu…?' – Babuji asked.

'Babuji, it is very kind of you to think of me…But I have my own problems…I help my mother in many household duties…and also I do not like the milk here. I like Gangi's milk only…'

'Who is Gangi?'

'Gangi is our cow.'

'Oh yes! I have seen a cow in your house! Don't worry! We can arrange to bring Gangi here.'

'Gangi cannot come alone. If she comes, Golu will also come with her.'

'Now who is Golu?'

'Golu is her calf'

Yes-Yes…Golu should also come with Gangi – what else, Raghu? You should make a list of things you need from your house. I will send your Rammu Mama to go to Nandanpur and bring Gangi and Golu along with your mother here with whatever you need…'

'Mother will come here?'

'I think, she will come… if Gangi comes.'

'Yes, she will come…' Raghu said, 'But how will you arrange all this?'

'I can arrange all this within three hours. Do you know why I am doing this, Raghu? Because Manavi has become a great hit! Look what the newspapers are saying about her!'

Babuji then placed two local dailies before Raghu. 'Open at the third page' – he said – 'The news of Vidisha is there…. See your photograph and Manavi's.'

Raghu scrolled through the pages of the newspaper. On the third page he was surprised to see his photo with Manavi! – 'Oh, this is Manavi and me!' - He exclaimed 'Look Manavi, your photograph has appeared in the newspaper!'

Manavi was biting a myrobalan fruit. All her attention was focused on the fruit. She took a bite and with her eyes half closed said – 'This fruit is tasty…'

'Manavi, I am showing you your photo and you are not seeing that!' – Raghu said.

'What is that to me?'- Manavi said and again took a bite.

At this moment, Ravindra joined them. 'Ravi Babu, our Raghu wants to learn spoken English.' Babuji told him - 'You make him an expert at English speaking in a week. Canyou do that?'

'Oh sure, sure!' Ravindra said, 'We start our first lesson today itself. I have a seven day course, which can be finished in a week.'

'Raghu, our company is here only for this week. You stay with us this week. We will not charge anything for tutoring you and the training you get with Ravindra will make you a man of this world.' Babuji told Raghu.

Raghu started laughing with joy. Kalanath was giving instructions to Ramsevak for going to Nandanpur and bringing Suhagini Devi, with Gangi and Golu from there. –'Maamaa, I will come with you to bring mother here.' – Raghu said.

If you go to Nandanpur', Babuji said, 'you will miss your first lesson with Ravindra. He is free only in the morning. Then he has to prepare for the afternoon show.'

Kalanath arranged for a truck. Raghu was looking pensive when the truck departed with Ramsevak seated on the front seat with the driver. Putting his hand on his shoulder, Ravindra said – 'Raghu, come, I can spare some time to coach you just now. After that I will get busy.'

17

Raghu was waiting for lunch. Suddenly Manavi shouted – 'Hurrah! Mother is here!'

Raghu ran to embrace his mother. Holding Manavi in her arms, Suhagini Devi asked – 'How are you, my daughter?'

'I am fine!' Manavi said.

After that Suhagini Devi caressed Raghu. Raghu said – 'Mother, I was longing for you. Good that you came. We will live here together in this circus company. There is a good tent. Everything is there!'

'I cannot leave Nandanpur' – Suhagini Devi said,'and I will have to stay with Gangi and Rammu...'

'But Mother, there is arrangement for Gangi here—'

'No, Raghu! I can't stay here.'

Ramsevak said – 'Didi, shall I take Gangi and Golu up to the turning of our house. The truck will not go inside the lane.'

A new chapter began in Raghu's life from that day. He would occasionally go to visit his mother at Mamaji's house Suhagini Devi came over twice during that week to see the show. She loved Manavi's performance. Raghu was taking his daily lessons in English speaking with Ravindra.

New dialogues between Manavi and Raghu were added for their show in the circus. The people of Vidisha were overwhelmed by their performance. Everybody was talking about a female swan speaking in human voice. Every sentence spoken by Manavi aroused their curiosity and thrilled the audience. The dialogues between Raghu and Manavi proceeded like this–

'Manavi, will you marry me...'

'No-No, I cannot marry you…'

'Why not, Manavi?'

'Because you men are cheats. You bring a co-wife.

'I will purchase a sari for you.'

'What will I do with a sari? I don't wear saris.'

In the evening show of the third day, Raghu forgot his lines- "I will purchase a sari for you." Ravindra immediately handled the situation and coming forward he asked Manavi – 'My dear Madam, when will I get married?'

'You should pose this question before your beloved.' – Manavi said.

People were surprised at her retort. – 'See, she knows everything. She is divine. She is an incarnation of Saraswati!' – some members of the audience were saying. The children were laughing. Ladies were blushing at the dialogues of Manavi. 'She is very mischievous!', an old lady remarked.

One week passed in Vidisha. Every day the crowd increased. Kalanath realized that this was all because of Manavi's item. He wanted to extend his stay, but the district administration did not permit it.

Raghu had now become fluent in English. He could talk with Maria without any hesitation. There were three girls from Russia in the company. They did not know Hindi. Raghu made friends with one of them. She was Valentina. It was because of Valentina that he practiced English speech with more concentration. Valentina curiously listened to the conversation between Manavi and Raghu during the circus shows. She could not understand what they talked, and asked Raghu one day what Manavi said and what he had asked her. She laughed when Raghu told her about his conversation with Manavi. Raghu felt as if several cuckoos were cooing in his ears when she laughed.

Kalanath got Suhagini Devi to sign an agreement for three months. He would pay a salary of three thousand rupees to her for Raghu working in his circus. He also cleared the complete payment of nine thousand rupees in advance. Suhagini Devi was overwhelmed with happiness. —With this amount I will get the roof of the house at Nandanpur repaired and will buy one more cow' – she thought.

At Nandanpur, Raghu had already become a celebrity. Sharda Prasad, the principal of his school gave him special leave and promised to allow him to appear in the examination when he returned back to Nandanpur after three months.

The company was now all set to go to Bharatpur. Suhagini Devi was to return to Nandanpur with Gangi and Golu. Raghu, Manavi and Ramsevak were accompanying them.

At the time of her departure from Vidisha, Suhagini Devi again and again reminded Ramsevak – 'Rammu, keep an eye on Raghu! He is very mischievous…'

Ramsevak was a happy man now. Babuji had made him a regular employee of the company with a fixed monthly salary. He was made in charge of the mess.

18

Next week, the company reached Bharatpur. Manavi was anxious to go to the sanctuary to see if the swans of her group had arrived there. But Babuji would not allow Raghu and her to go out. 'Raghu! it is for her safety and yours' – Babuji said when Raghu protested.

Raghu was unhappy over these security arrangements. 'When will we take Manavi to the bird sanctuary?' – he asked Babuji.

'After three months.'

'Why three months?'

'Look Raghu, your mother has signed a contract with me. For three months, you have to present your show with Manavi everyday when the circus is going on. If you violate this contract, you and your mother will beput in jail.

Raghu was shocked. He was going at Babuji. He never thought that Babuji could be so cruel. Then tears appeared in his eyes. With a chocked throat he said — 'You have already put me and Manavi in jail.'

Suddenly Kalanath softened. He placed his hand on Raghu's shoulder and said in a tender re-assuring voice – 'Raghu, don't be cross with me!'

Raghu was not appeased. He said annoyingly – 'OK, you do whatever you want to. I will go and leave Manavi at the birds sanctuary. You have spoiled my life for your selfish motive. Your circus is now running because of Manavi – I know it. I have left my school and Manavi her joy for your circus. She is not very happy here… If she is not happy, I cannot force her to perform at the show.'

Kalanath stared at Raghu. He did not expect Raghu to be so tough. He understood how important Raghu had become for his circus. He said in a more pleasing voice – 'Raghu, I am your friend and not an enemy. I have talked to a good teacher here at Bharatpur for your coaching with him. That will cover the loss of your studies at Nandanpur school and the principal of your school will allow you to appear in the exams. You have brought your books here, you can continue with your studies here. I acknowledge that you and Manavi have instilled a new life in our circus. But I have also helped your mother and your Mama. They are very happy. You should be proud of the fact that you are helping them. And also, please try to understand. It is not simply my gain, it is your gain too. You are becoming famous day by day. You have become a hero. Manavi's posters with you are displayed in the markets, on the streets and cross-roads. You are a celebrity now.'

'But the contract did not say that you will put her in a cage with this security.'

Thieves and dacoits may steal or abduct Manavi. This is the report given to me by the police department.'

Raghu bowed his head.

In Bharatpur, people were enamored with Manavi. They even tried to see Manavi apart from the circus shows. They thought that some saint has incarnated in the form of a swan. Sometimes some mischievous boys would cross the barricade and try to come close to Manavi. Ravindra would rush to drive them away with a stick. His stick would make a strange cracking noise when swung in the air.

At last, three months passed at Bharatpur. The members of the circus company were happy. The city of Agra was very near and Delhi was also not very far away. There was no show on Wednesdays. One Wednesday, Babuji made a trip to Agra. They also purchased ten quintals of sugarcane for the elephants there and brought the load in a truck. Manavi liked the petha (a sweet) from Agra. Babuji was also assuring Raghu and Manavi that he was inquiring at the Bharatpur sanctuary almost daily to know whether the swans from the Himalayas have arrived.

Raghu was now reconciled to Babuji. He appreciated his efforts at running such a big circus company. Kalanath also appreciated Raghu's efforts to run his show with Manavi. Raghu had now become a very good performer, he could invent new dialogues, could amuse the audience. A kind of understanding developed between Babuji and Raghu and they were now friends.

One day Kalanath told Raghu the whole story of his life. Raghu was moved to hear the tale of his suffering and sacrifice for the circus. Babuji is great – he thought – he did not marry that girl of a wealthy merchant. He loves everybody in the circus, he cares for all the animals here.

Raghu's friendship with Valentina was also developing into a strong bond. Valentina was a jolly girl. But she was curious about Manavi, and kept on asking Raghu what Manavi was saying. Raghu would translate Manavi's speech into English for her. 'Why do you ask her – Will you marry her?' She is a bird, you know, you cannot marry a bird…'- Valentina told Raghu.

'I know, I know – this is just for the show' – Raghu would say laughing -- 'The public is amused…'

'She is just a bird …she does not even understand what marriage is. In Russia also we have talking birds. They just repeat what we say…they don't have brains.'

'I did not train Manavi. In fact, she has trained me' – Raghu said.

Kalanathhad again and again assured Raghu and Manavi that he was constantly making inquiries at the bird sanctuary of Bharatpur to confirm if the swans from Himalayas have arrived. Still there was no positive reply.

Three months were over. The circus made good income at Bharatpur. Babuji declared fifteen days' break. Ravindra said that he will go to Kolkata, and Maria wanted to go to Kerala. Valentina and other girls from Russia would be returning to their country. The term of their Visa would be over next week.

'Raghu, we are going to Delhi today and from there we will fly to Moscow,' Valentina said.

'When will you come to India again, Valentina?' Raghu asked anxiously.

I am not sure…it all depends on the contract between Moscow Circus Company and this circus company…our company is also thinking of exchanging the artists of this company.....You come to Moscow, Raghu! You will enjoy the performances in our company. We don't have any animals but our acrobats are very impressive.'

At this juncture, the other girls called Valentina as their vehicle for Delhi was ready to start and they had already boarded. Valentina said – 'OK, bye Raghu!' and ran to board the car.

'I will miss you!' – stretching her head out of the car window Valentina said. Her companions started laughing.

'I will also miss you very much' – Raghu tried to say, but the car had already moved away.

Raghu felt were lonely. He was missing his mother. 'Mama, let's go to Nandanpur now. I am sick of this circus business I will not come back' he was telling Ramsevak.

It was Sunday. Kalanath had given leave to all the employees of the company. They may rest or go for shopping or sightseeing. He also told Raghu – 'Let us go to the bird sanctuary today. We will confirm whether the swans of Manavi's group have arrived. If they are there, you may leave Manavi with them if she so wishes. I have made inquiries from the officers of the sanctuary repeatedly. There are swans there, but they are not sure if they have come from Himalayas. Salim Ali also says that the swans from Himalayas will not go the sanctuaries of northern India.'

19

The bird sanctuary at Bharatpur is very beautiful. Now it is called Keoladeo National Park and not only birds, all kinds of wild animals assemble here.

Manavi was not interested in seeing other animals. The moment they entered the main gate, she told Raghu – 'Raghu, you ask where the birds' section is, or you just ask where the swans are – and we will proceed to that sight. There is no point in roaming aimlessly.'

They inquired about the place where they could find swans and proceeded to that place. Various types of birds were there. The cranes were standing motionless in a pool. In between they would swiftly pluck a fish and then again they would stand erect and still. Some vultures and kites were also there.

As they moved on, looking for the group of swans, Raghu was amazed to see the wonderful and variegated world of birds. There was a big white cock and parrots of diverse colours.

Many swans were floating in a pond. Raghu showed them to Manavi and asked her – 'Manavi, do you recognize them?

Manavi said in a sad tone – 'No, they do not belong to our tribe.'

They were tired after roaming in the area. Manavi said – 'Raghu, the swans of my group have not come here. I am feeling sick. Let us go back.'

Babuji said sympathetically – 'Manavi, my daughter! I thought that we will somehow find your colleagues here. Are you sure that none of them is here?'

Manavi said –'Don't worry Babuji. It is my fate.'

Kalanath became very emotional. He said – 'I am thinking of releasing all the animals in my circus. Nobody should suffer, everyone should enjoy freedom. Everyone should be free.'

Raghu was surprised. – 'How will you run the circus then?' – he asked.

'Raghu, the days of circus are over.'

They had now comeout of the sanctuary. There was a big temple outside. They went to have a 'darshan'. There was a big statue of Lord Shiva in the temple. Raghu prayed for the happiness of Manavi and his mother. Babuji stood with folded hands before the statue with his eyes closed.

Then they returned back to their camp.

20

Next day, Raghu returned to Nandanpur with Ramsevak. Suhagini Devi was overjoyed to see Raghu and Manavi. The examinations were drawing near. Raghu immersed himself in his studies.

Manavi was not feeling good at Nandanpur now. She looked depressed. She did not talk to Raghu also. Raghu used to narrate his experiences in the circus to his mother and his friends. He was all praise for Manavi. 'She is simply a genius' – he said. But nothing could please Manavi.

Raghu asked her – 'Manavi! why are you so sad?'

Manavi said – 'I am a bird, and you are a human being. Very soon you will become a man of this world. You will not leave this world for me. I left my world for you.'

Raghu said – 'I am also not very happy at Nandanpur. After examinations my friends will be leaving Nandanpur.'

Nandanpur was changing. A highway was being constructed under the Prime Minister's scheme of building roads in rural areas. Many people of the village got jobs in this project. Some young men got jobs at Vidisha and Bhopal. The farmers were desisting from agriculture.

One day Raghu said – 'Manavi, will you learn the Gayatri Mantra? I have practiced it with the priest in the temple...'

Manavi said – 'OK, I will try to learn it.'

Every day he would then chant Gayatri mantra before Manavi many times. Manavi would repeat after him.

Suhagini Devi was also worried about Manavi. She said – 'My daughter, you should listen to the Ramayana...that will give you solace....'

She would read *Ramcharitmanas* daily. Manavi would listen to the *chaupayies,* sitting beside her.

Five years passed by. Babuji would call Raghu and Manavi twice or thrice in a year for giving shows in the circus. Raghu was paid handsome wages. Babuji also offered him a permanent job in the circus, but Raghu did not want to quit school and Suhagini Devi also did not want him to join the circus permanently. They now had a pucca house. The dairy of Samata Prasad had closed sometimes back, Suhagini Devi meanwhile started her own dairy. She supplied milk far and wide, even up to Vidisha. She was assisted by Ramsevak in this business. He was now married and had opened a grocery shop at Vidisha.

Raghu cleared his class XII exams this year. What next? There was no college at Nandanpur. Some of his classmates were going to Vidisha for further studies. Raghu did not want to join college. 'I want to do some job' – he told Manavi and his mother. He missed the circus. 'If there is nothing else I will join Babuji's circus!' - he declared.

This year he had not gone for performance at the circus because of his board examinations.

One day he was surprised to receive a letter from Valentina. He told Manavi – 'Manavi, do you know who has sent me this letter? It is from Valentina!'

'You will sometime meet her' Manavi said.

Most of Raghu's friends had left Nandanpur. Sheela was married this year. Shravan went to Delhi and Devesh had opened a cycle shop at Nandanpur. Raghu went to Vidisha many times these days. Mama and Mamiji were pleased to see him. Mama said– 'Why don't you move to Vidisha with Didi? You can study here or do some business.'

Raghu used to read a lot. He brought books from Vidisha. In the office of Gram Panchayat at Nandanpur, a computer system was installed. But there was no operator, the representatives of the Panchayat did not know how to operate the system. Raghu did some office work for them and in his free time he read a lot of books on the internet there.

'You enjoyed your work at the circus, isn't it?!' – Suhagini Devi told him one day – 'If they call you again, why don't you join them?'

What to do mother! I do not know where Babuji is. There is no contact with him for the past one year. Last time he took me to Odissa. We gave performances at Puri and Bhubaneshwar. There also people were pleased with Manavi's performance. Babuji had said—'Raghu, you should now devote yourself to your studies. You should at least have a School Board Certificate. When your examinations are over, I will come to take you. I want you to join our circus on full time basis. You can learn many things here. You will become a man of the world then!'

The month of June was nearing. Raghu was waiting for a call from Kalanath.

One morning he was brushing his teeth when he heard someone call on the door – 'Raghu! Raghu!!'

Raghu was surprised. Who can it be so early in the morning?

'Babuji has come! Babuji has come!!' Manavi announced.

Raghu washed his mouth and came out hurriedly. There was a car standing at his door. The car seemed to be Babuji's. But where was he?

Then his eyes rested on the neem tree. Manavi was sitting on a low branch there and Babuji was talking to her.

'Oh! Babuji! When did you come?'Raghu touched his feet and asked.

'I reached just now! Look what Manavi says! She says she is bored with Nandanpur!'

'I don't know what I should do for Manavi!' – Raghu said in a sad tone.

'Come inside, we will discuss things with Didi!'– Babuji said, and he came inside as if the house belonged to him. Suhagini Devi saw him entering the drawing room from the kitchen and she immediately came out to meet him, saying – 'Oh Kala Babu! You have come after so many days!'

Kalanath touched her feet and asked – 'Everything is alright, Didi?'

'Everything is alright. How is it that the sun rose in the west today!' – Suhagini Devi said.

'What should I do, Didi? I always missed you and Raghu. But for the past six months, I could not get a moment's rest.

The boat of our circus is sinking. I do not know how long it will survive!'

'We will not allow the boat of our circus to sink!' Raghu said.

'We will not allow the boat of our circus to sink!' – Manavi repeated his words. Suhagini Devi and Kalanath laughed. Then Kalanath proceeded to narrate the tale of his woes. He had to dispose of all the wild animals in possession of the circus company. Ravindra and Maria were married now and were settled at Kolkata. Both of them had quit Natraj Circus Company. Kalanath had desperately tried to sustain the company. Now there was a good development – he had entered into a contract with the Moscow Circus Company.

Meanwhile Suhagini Devi had gone inside the kitchen to put a pot of water to boil on the gas oven for preparing tea. She had installed a gas plant fuelled by cow dung at the backyard of her house and did her cooking on the gas-chulha.

She was listening to every word of Kalanath with attention. 'Kalababu – you appear somewhat tired! I had asked you to marry a good girl. Look! Rammu is younger than you. He has married and is well settled – thanks to the amount given by you – he runs his kirana shop properly at Vidisha.' She said in a loud voice from the kitchen.

Kalanath laughed and said, 'The contract with Moscow Circus Company provides for exchange of five artists each between the two companies. They will send five artists from their side and we will send five artists to them twice a year for three months.

'Will Valentina come to India in the exchange?' Raghu wanted to ask. At this juncture, Suhagini Devi came in with two mugs of tea in a tray.

Suddenly Kalanath asked Raghu – 'Raghu, will you come to Moscow with me?'

Raghu was startled. – 'Me? Moscow? What will I do there?'

'Valentina is there!' – Kalanath said and laughed.

'You are joking!' – Raghu said blushingly. After a deep breath, he again said – 'I have neither passport nor visa.'

'I will arrange for everything. Don't worry. There is bright future for a young man like you in Russia. But we have to ask Manavi whether she is willing to go to Russia?'

'Manavi, would you like to come to Russia with me and Babuji?' – Raghu asked Manavi.

'Yes, I would love to go to Russia.'

'Poor Manavi! She is so disgusted with our village that she is willing even to go to such a distant country like Russia' – Raghu said with pity – 'All this is because of me…five years have gone by! I often think of that fateful day when Manavi overstayed because of me and the members of her group left.'

'Don't worry, everything will be alright! Let us plan our trip then' – Kalanath said. He then started talking with Suhagini Devi. She agreed that Raghu liked to work in the circus; he could learn many things there. Kalanath said that Raghu would be an asset to his circus company. He has proved to be very helpful. 'Didi, if you allow me, we will enter into an agreement for one year initially' – he said – 'only this month five persons are to go to Russia for working with the Moscow Circus Company. Raghu and Manavi can accompany us…'

'It is alright… you can get him to do any work in the circus except running the bike in the death well…that is dangerous.'

'Don't worry,I will not ask him to do any such thing. Raghu's favourite item is his dialogue with Manavi. Everybody likes it. I hope people in Russia will also enjoy it!'

Raghu became very sad. 'How about mother?' – he said with a heavy heart – 'I don't want to leave her here for such a long time.'

'Don't worry about me, Raghu!' Suhagini Devi said – 'Rammu quite often visits Nandanpur now for our dairy business. In fact, our dairy is thriving because of him. He will take care of me. My Bhabhi is a very good lady… She also likes to be in my company.'

'Raghu, contact Ramsevak bhai. Ask him to come here.' Kalanath said.

'Babuji! You are tired!' – Raghu said – 'Take rest. Stay with us at least for one day. We now have a guest room. I will get it ready for you within five minutes'

'Thank you, Raghu! Go, prepare for your trip with me, we will go tomorrow.'

Raghu contacted his Mama, Ramasevak over phone. 'Babuji is here! He wants to see you!' he told him.

Ramsevak came in the afternoon. After hearing from Raghu and Kalanath, he said – 'I am thinking of moving to Nandanpur. I can work better for milk supply to Vidisha and even up to Bhopal from here. Raghu's Mamiji will live here, she will take care of my Didi.'

21

Next day Raghu reached Delhi with Manavi and Babuji. Kalanath took both of them to the house of his elder brother, Bholanath.

Pankaj, Bholanath's son was charmed by Manavi. He insisted that the bird should be given to him, he wanted to play with her.

Manavi told him –' I have to go to Russia. When I come back, I will stay with you.'

'Is it a promise?' Pankaj asked.

Manavi laughed..

'Look, she is not making the promise, that means she will not come back to me!' Pankaj said and started howling. Bhamati, his mother scolded him.

Next week, Manavi and Raghu reached Moscow with Kalanath. There were three more persons with them – Roli and Shankari with their father Satyadev. They gave the show of walking on the rope. They had gone to Russia earlier also for their performance.

They found Moscow very beautiful. The audience went gaga over the performance of Roli and Shankari. Manavi was not her usual self on the first day. Contrary to expectations, her performance with Raghu did not go well. The audience failed to understand what she was talking. Many of them said that a bird cannot speak like this, it is all fake.

Raghu met Valentina after a long time, She had become a beautiful young lady with a glowing complexion. To Raghu she appeared like a moving image of gold. He stared at her in amazement the moment his eyes fell on her.

'Hi Raghu, you have become as tall as a tree!' – Glancing at him with her eyes wide open, Valentina exclaimed.

Raghu felt shy. He wanted to say – 'But you look so beautiful and charming!' His lips quivered to utter – 'Oh no!' awkwardly and then he fell silent.

The show went very well after the next day. People also started appreciating Manavi. Next week the circus company moved to St. Petersburg. Raghu liked it even better than Moscow. Meanwhile, Manavi had picked up one or two Russian words. The audience enjoyed her saying, 'Das-Veedhaniiiyaa!'

'Can this bird chant some mantra in Sanskrit?'– An old man arose from the audience to ask on the third day in St. Petersburg when Raghu was presenting Manavi's show.

Valentina was standing with Raghu as interpreter. She translated what the old man had asked. 'Manavi, chant the Gayatri mantra!' Raghu told Manavi.

'*OM Bhuur bhuvah svah tat savitur varenyam bhargo devasya dhiimahi dhiyo yo nah prachodayaat*'. —Manavi chanted the entire Gayantri mantra.

The old man was very happy. He gave a standing ovation for Manavi.

They had only one show in the afternoon on all the days,except the weekends. That too only for two hours. The rest of the day Raghu spent in sightseeing with Valentina. Kalanath wanted to take rest. Shankari and Roli had formed a deep friendship with two acrobat girls in the Moscow theatre company. They were practicing their art and making them learn rope walking. Raghu, Valentina and Manavi often went sightseeing. They saw the Czar's palace. The city's numerous canals provided pleasure trips in beautiful boats.

22

It was their last day in St. Petersburg. Next day in the morning they were to leave for Moscow. From Moscow they were to leave for Delhi the next day. There was no show today.

Early in the morning Babuji telephoned from his room to say that he would be sitting for some time in the lawn of the swimming pool,Raghu could come there if he wishes. Raghu came down in the lobby with Manavi. We will go to the swimming pool area now – Raghu was saying. Suddenly Manavi got herself free from his hands and flying in the lobby she went close to a lady sitting with a man on the sofa, busy in some discussion with him. Raghu shouted – 'Manavi! Manavi!! What are you doing? You should not disturb other people!'– Saying this, he ran to Manavi.

Manavi was sitting on the hand rest beside the lady. The lady touched her gently. She said to Raghu – 'Lovely bird. Is she yours?'

'Yes' – Raghu said – 'Sorry, she disturbed you!'

'No, no not at all! ' – the lady protested – 'In fact, we had finished our discussion. By the way, you are from India?'

'Yes!' – Raghu said –'And you?'

'I am also from India. I run my business from Delhi.'

The man sitting with the lady got up and said – 'OK, we have finished our business talk. I will contact you. See you again!'

'Raghu, ask her to come with us to the swimming pool!'– suddenly Manavi told Raghu.

The lady was astonished. 'Did you hear?' - She asked Raghu.'This bird was chattering something.'

'She is a talking bird. She speaks to me in my language.'

'And what did she say?'

'I am sorry. Please don't take it otherwise. She does not mean anything…'

'Did she say something about me?'

'She wants you to join both of us. I am going to the swimming pool area…'

'Oh, no problem! I have done my business here. I can spend some moments with you and her.'

Saying this she got up and moved towards the rear of the hotel with Raghu and Manavi.

The moment they reached the lawns around the swimming pool, Manavi said, 'I am going to Babuji!'

Leaving Raghu with the lady, she flew towards the corner where Kalanath was sitting.

'Nice, jolly bird! How beautiful she looks when she flies!' The lady said, 'but where has she gone?'

'She has gone to meet Babuji, who has come with us from India. Please come, I will introduce you to him.'

As soon as the lady saw Kalanath, she stood aghast. 'What happened? Please come!', Raghu said.

Kalanath noticed her and stood standstill. They stood with their eyes fixed on each other for several moments. Raghu was embarrassed. 'Babu ji, It is Manavi's fault. She brought Madam with us here!', he somehow managed to say.

'Manavi can do miracles.' Kalanath said in an astonished manner.

Finally the lady spoke to Kalanath – 'Hello, do you recognize me?'

'Vandana!....How are you here?'Kalanath muttered in a choked voice.

So this was Vandana! – Raghu thought. She is the lady because of whom Babuji did not marry till now.

'Thank God! You still remember me and my name!' Vandana said and laughed. Raghu observed that her voice was also choked.

'He is Raghu and that bird is Manavi' – Kalanath introduced Raghu and Manavi to Vandana.

'I met them in the lobby' – Vandana said – 'In fact, Manavi – this bird, has brought me here.'

'Manavi always does sensible things at the right moment. She is a great artist in our circus. She talks in our language.'

' Your circus is going on well?' – Vandana asked.

'Not so well. We met because of the circus in India and we have again met here because I am here to give my show for the Moscow Circus.'

'Oh! Now I remember. I read in the newspaper about a talking female swan from India giving shows for the Moscow Circus. I could never imagine that you might be with this group.'

'I also could never imagine that I will meet you here. Please sit here Vandana! I need to talk to you. After all these years...' Kalanath spoke with a quiver in his voice.

'Raghu, let us go! Let them talk to each other!' – Manavi said.

Raghu moved to the other side of the swimming pool with Manavi.

Kalanath and Vandana spoke to one another for quite sometime. Raghu was roaming around the pond with Manavi. He glanced at Kalanath and Vandana at intervals. Both of them were looking at each other with a glow in their eyes. They seemed to be completely lost in some other world.

Vandana was telling Kalanath about her garment business. The garment industry she has been running had prospered and was expanding outside India too. In fact, she was visiting Russia to explore the possibility of opening a showroom in Moscow. She was staying in some other hotel, but had an appointment with an industrialist here. Her father was ailing. He could not walk, but looked after the business from his wheelchair. Two years back he had told Vandana – 'I give up my vow to marry you to a young man who agrees to become a 'gharjamai'. If you still like to marry that circus manager, please do so!'

'But how can I leave my father at this stage?' – Vandana said – 'His health is not good...'- saying this Vandana's eyes were filled with tears.

After Vandana had left, Kalanath told everything to Raghu and declared – 'Raghu, I am leaving the circus for Vandana! I will also change the date of my departure from Moscow.

Vandana will leave for Delhi next week…I will come with her. You and the others go to Delhi tomorrow. You are intelligent, you will be able to manage everything. Please go with these two girls, Roli and Shankari and their father. I will give you enough money to manage the affairs. Meet my elder brother Bholanath in Delhi and tell him that your Babuji is going to marry Vandana Bajaj…he will understand. You will now be the manager of Natraj Circus Company. We will complete the formalities when I come back to Delhi.'

Raghu felt as if he had fallen from the sky. 'Babuji! Don't leave us!' – he said with a choked voice. – 'How can I run the circus…It is a very complicated thing!'

'Don't worry, Raghu! I will always be with you. In fact, I will stay with you in Delhi until I marry Vandana and go to stay with the Bajajs. I assumed the charge of this circus when I was your age and you are more competent than me.'

Raghu was excited and yet sad. Kalanath tried to re-assure him. He also called Roli, Shankari and Satyadev and told them of his plans.

In the evening he left for the hotel where Vandana was staying. Vandana had booked a room for him there.

'Manavi, what should we do now? Babuji has left us! There is nothing to do now. I have packed my baggage.' – Raghu said.

'We can go for an outing…'

'Yes, we must go for an outing' – saying this Valentina entered their room.

-'What a pleasure!' – Raghu said – 'I was just remembering you! We are going to leave tomorrow.'

'If you don't have any other program, we can go to a sanctuary nearby. There is a river called Suten… There are several picnic spots on the bank of this river and the trip finally ends in a big sanctuary. We can go there.'

'OK, I would love to go there. How about you Manavi?'

'I also would like to go.' – Manavi said.

Satyadev was taking rest in the room. Roli and Shankari had gone shopping in a nearby shopping mall.

23

They reached a valley with the river flowing around. The valley was echoing with continuous chirping of birds. Manavi appeared to be excited. She was talking all the time saying things which neither Raghu nor Valentina could understand. But they were enjoying the trip. Raghu and Valentina were laughing whenever Manavi tried to say something and she became incoherent.

'Manavi, there are swans!' – suddenly Raghu cried.

'You are right! Swans are there and they are of my breed–' Manavi said excitedly

'Manavi! Manavi!!'- suddenly Manavi heard a call.

'Raghu! Leave me! I am going!'

'Where are you going Manavi?

'Anant! It is his call! He is asking me to come!'

'But where is he? I do not see him anywhere!'

'You were not able to see him at Nandanpur also. He remains invisible for you people. But I can recognize him. I see him, I hear his voice…He is there on the other side of the fountain!'

'Manavi! Manavi! I can see you, can you see me?'Anant called out to Manavi from the other side of the fountain.

'Anant! I can see you, I can also hear you!'– Manavi said.

Raghu glanced at the other side of the fountain. Yes! There were some swans over there.

Manavi was fluttering her feathers. 'Please let me go!'she again told Raghu.

'Raghu! Let Manavi go if she wants to.' Valentina said.

'You are going Manavi? You are leaving us?' – Raghu said in a sad tone.

'What to do Raghu! Anant is calling me! Once I had ignored his call and have suffered because of that.'

'Go, Manavi, go! You belong to your group of swans!' Raghu said in a choked voice and released Manavi.

Manavi flew to the other side of the fountain. Anant was really there. 'What a surprise, Anant, you being here!'

–'I am equally surprised to see you here, Manavi!' Anant said.

Manavi told him everything – her joining the circus with Raghu and then her trip to Russia.

Anant also briefed her on what had transpired since they got separated. 'During the last five years we have stayed at many places. We could not return to Nandanpur due to many hurdles on the path of return. We went to the Himalayas last year. But Himalaya has changed. The mountaineers try to climb the peaks and they throw edibles and other things on the way. The foul smell of these things has polluted the area. The ice is melting. We flew to the other side of the Himalayas in search of a better place. Then there was a massive snowfall on the way and some of the members who were with me in the journey died.. Grandfather Suchanchu is no more, Dalbhya, Shanku and Uddanda also died. Pavani and Tandya survive. They are here with me… It is good to stay here… but I was missing you, Manavi!'

Tears rolled down Manavi's eyes.– 'What a loss!', she said with a sigh, 'Grandpa and Shanku and others – all have gone…'

Anant said, 'Manavi, I was cross with you that day when you took long to return, and we were leaving Nandanpur. I did not wait for you. I should have waited. You delayed for a good cause. You have helped that boy, Raghu. I was jealous of him. But you were concerned about him as he was innocent. I see he is a man of the world now!'

'No, Anant! It was my fault. I forgot you and our group due to my involvement with Raghu. He was actually hungry and I helped him by dropping fruits from a mango tree that day.'

Epilogue

Valentina held Raghu's hand and told him—'Come, Raghu! Manavi will not return now. Let us go.'

Raghu called out desperately—'Manavi, please come back!'

Manavi flew to the other side with Anant. She said—'Raghu, you have been very kind to me. You have saved me from many dangers in the world of human beings. Thank you for all that…Now I return to my world. Don't be sad—you will always remain happy from now onwards…'

'Good bye, Manavi!' Raghu said with a heavy heart.

He then moved from the spot with Valentina holding her hand and now he did not look back.